Promoting Social Competence

G. Gordon Williamson,
Ph.D., OTR, FAOTA

Wilma J. Dorman, OTR/L

Therapy Skill Builders®

from ⓟThe Psychological Corporation
A Harcourt Assessment Company

Library of Congress Cataloging-in-Publication Data

Williamson, G. Gordon
  Promoting social competence / G. Gordon Williamson, Wilma J. Dorman.
    p. cm.
Includes bibliographical references.
  ISBN 0-7616-0216-X (Pbk.)
  1. Social skills. 2. Social skills in children. I. Dorman,
Wilma J. II. Title.

  HM691 D67 2002
  302.3'4—dc21

                                        2002015175

**Therapy
Skill Builders®**

from ⑫The Psychological Corporation
A Harcourt Assessment Company

076160216X

1 2 3 4 5 6 7 8 9 10 11 12 A B C D E

Printed in the United States of America.

Visit our Web site at www.PsychCorp.com

Published by Therapy Skill Builders,
19500 Bulverde Road,
San Antonio, TX 78259, USA, 1-800-872-1726

We dedicate this book to

Albert H. Dorman, Jr.

and

A. Georg Fleischer, M.D.

Acknowledgements

We wish to thank the children and families who have, over the years, taught us about the journey to achieve social competence. They continue to be our inspiration. The professional staff at OTR, Inc., in Blue Bell, Pennsylvania was instrumental in the ongoing development of our intervention frame of reference. They are committed to best practices and clinical creativity. We appreciate the special contributions of Tina Magliente, who provided technical and organizational support for the book.

This work was supported in part by grants from The Robert Wood Johnson Foundation and the Office of Special Education and Rehabilitation Services of the U.S. Department of Education (Project ERA #HO24P50085; Project BEAM #H324R980042). We are also grateful to Patricia Munday, Ed.D., director of the Pediatric Rehabilitation Department of the John F. Kennedy Medical Center in Edison, New Jersey, who unfailingly assisted this endeavor.

At key points in the development of the manuscript, Larry Edelman, M.S., and Linda Florey, Ph.D., OTR, were most generous with their time and talents. Larry reviewed the entire document and provided rich feedback about its organization and structure. Linda provided detailed reflections on our conceptual framework and content. We are deeply indebted to these gifted friends. Orna Azulay, M.A., CCC-SLP, reviewed the sections related to language and communication and offered helpful guidance.

We are also indebted to the gifted staff at Therapy Skill Builders. Pam Parmer provided computer assistance that was superb and timely. Connie Sabo, our copy editor, refined the text with professional skill and respect for the book's content. Editorial assistant Andrew Joyce provided the final editorial polish and worked closely with our gifted designer, Marian Zahora, to create a book design that is both elegant and accessible. Michelle Girard Rolfhus, our editorial project manager, made the publishing process a pleasure. She kept us on track in a firm but gentle manner. Terri Robertson, our acquisitions manager, understood and promoted the book from the start.

Al Dorman and Georg Fleischer were patient and encouraging during the long development of the book. They kept us focused and motivated.

Table of Contents

Preface

Promoting Social Competence is a practical resource for enhancing the social competence of children 3 to 12 years of age. It is based on a conceptual framework that addresses the major components of social competence: social and play behaviors; self-regulation; communication; prosocial skills; and social decision making. It emphasizes peer interaction within natural, age-appropriate activities as the major vehicle for effecting change; this approach is not a set curriculum but rather one tailored to the personal needs of each child in the major life contexts of family, school, and community.

This approach is appropriate both for children with identified disabilities and for children with possible disabilities currently unidentified by either a medical or educational system. This book is applicable for children who have mild to moderate social difficulties of varying etiologies including physical disability, learning disability, behavioral problems, language disorder, and severe developmental delay. The content is also relevant for enriching the social abilities of children who are developing at age-appropriate levels.

Promoting Social Competence was written for an interdisciplinary audience of service providers and administrators involved with children with identified social problems. The targeted disciplines come from the therapeutic, educational, and psychosocial fields. This book is appropriate for practitioners who work in school systems, hospitals, clinics, rehabilitation agencies, and community-based organizations. It is also appropriate for use by individuals who conduct sports, recreational, cultural, and leisure activities for children in summer camps, "Y" programs, Little League, Scouts, and neighborhood events. This information is also beneficial for students at colleges and universities who are in training to work with children, and for parents and family members who may find the content helpful in understanding the nature of their child's social development and in enhancing the child's interpersonal competence. Collaborative sharing by parents and professionals is particularly powerful in developing a complete view of a child's uniqueness and potential.

The approach detailed in these pages can be used in a variety of ways. Its primary purpose is to contribute to program planning for children with special developmental, behavioral, or learning needs in segregated or inclusive settings. Critical information is also provided on the assessment of social behavior and the intervention to foster it. The book can also be used to help the reader to design enriched social experiences for more typically developing children; indeed, one of the book's strengths is the detailed description of strategies and activities to promote social competence that have been successful in the field. The content is useful also for those providing indirect services such as administrators, supervisors, and consultants.

The scope of the book is broad in its coverage but explicit in describing the knowledge and skills required by the practitioner; the book initially can be used to generate ideas on how to work with children and then revisited periodically to address specific topics related to new clinical challenges.

The text is divided into five sections. Section One, Setting the Stage, defines social competence, describing the most common intervention programs that are designed to address this domain. The frame of reference developed by the authors is then presented with an accompanying discussion of the characteristics of children with social challenges. Section

Two, Conceptual Framework, explores the nature of social interaction and the components of social competence. Section Three, Characteristics of Children With Social Difficulties, discusses some of the social competence issues that affect children and presents common behavioral profiles. Section Four, Assessment, addresses the assessment of children's capabilities in the major components of social competence, focusing on methods of data collection, and describes approaches to setting individual and group intervention goals. Finally, Section Five, Intervention, discusses group program structure: its operation and activity analysis in planning intervention.

Setting the Stage

Social Competence

I was just turning 6 and was excited about my first birthday party. Mom invited everyone from my class. But the day of the party no one showed. I don't know why! It still bothers me a lot. — Laura, age 9

Jared is always annoying the other children. I wish I knew how to help him make a place with them — and help them see his delightful qualities. — Teacher

---

No matter how many times I reached out to other mothers — to go for a cup of coffee or to have their kids over to play with mine so we could just visit together — no one took me up on my offers. It was as if I were being punished for Ryan's behavior. They saw him as a bad kid and I was a bad mother. — Mother

---

Overview of Social Competence

The social world of children can be one of great joy and fulfillment. It can also be one of pain and embarrassment for those children who have a history of being rejected or ignored by their peers. *Promoting Social Competence* provides a practical resource for designing and conducting multifaceted programs aimed at enhancing the social well-being of children ages 3 to 12. This chapter defines social competence, differentiates between it and social skills, and discusses social problems often seen in children, particularly children with special needs. The two most common intervention approaches used in social skills training, the instructional approach and the social problem-solving approach, are described and their strengths and limitations are delineated. Finally, our activity-based approach is introduced and its unique features highlighted.

To introduce the concept of social competence let's look at this vignette of a little girl named Jenny.

> Jenny, who is 10 years old, was assigned to a small group within her class to design a poster. Jenny is terrific in art and this was a favorite project for her; she could immediately visualize the finished product, so she started giving directions to everyone. In her excitement, Jenny became intense and bossy; when other children in the group tried to contribute ideas and asked to do the jobs they liked, Jenny ignored them and plowed ahead with her own vision. The other group members became angry and told Jenny they did not like her idea. Finally, the other children stopped working with her. Jenny went home and told her mother that the kids in school were picking on her.

In her enthusiasm, Jenny did not recognize that the project required the collaborative efforts of all of the group members; consequently, she did not use such social skills as listening, sharing, taking turns, and reading the feelings of others. The unfortunate outcome of this episode could have been avoided had Jenny perceived the negative reactions of the other group members and adjusted her approach accordingly. She would have been more persuasive and effective if she had expressed her enthusiasm in a way that was less bossy and more open to the suggestions and ideas of the other children.

Instead, what did happen? Unable to discriminate the demands of the social setting and excited about doing her favorite project, Jenny ignored the expectation that everyone would collaborate on the poster and instead focused solely on the steps needed to complete the project. Because of this poor beginning, Jenny was unable to determine the verbal and nonverbal skills necessary to successfully manage the situation. Because of her highly focused agenda, she did not notice or respond to the needs and overtures of the others. Because she did not appreciate the desires of the other children, Jenny did not execute verbal and nonverbal skills in a fluid manner appropriate to social norms and she exhibited few of the behaviors that would have helped her achieve their cooperation, such as active listening and turn taking. Jenny persisted in dominating the project and was unable to perceive the reactions of others accurately; consequently, she made no attempt to adjust to this feedback. As a result, the group members withdrew from the project, leaving Jenny with no understanding of why they withdrew. Her faulty interpretation was that she was a victim and the others were picking on her.

Jenny's story illustrates an experience common for many children in the classroom, in the cafeteria, and on the playing field. When such experiences occur over and over again, a child may develop a sense of inadequacy and frustration. Over time, poor self-esteem may emerge and the child may come to view the world as hostile and rejecting. To assist children like Jenny a practitioner needs to understand the nature of social competence, be able to recognize deficits, and be able to apply a wide variety of intervention strategies. The classic definition of social competency formulated by Schumaker and Hazel (1984) is particularly useful because it delineates the broad elements that make up social competence. In this definition, social competence reflects the child's ability to:

- discriminate the demands of the social setting;
- determine the verbal and nonverbal skills necessary for the situation;
- execute those skills in a fluid manner appropriate to social norms;
- effectively perceive the reactions of others; and
- adjust to this feedback.

This definition clearly describes the active transaction between the individual and the social environment. The ability to initiate and maintain effective relationships is seen in the dynamic exchange. The environmental context is critical in establishing the expectation for appropriate social behaviors and the social context is the stage upon which life is played out. A child's day involves many scenes, from the privacy of the bedroom, to the bus ride to school, and on through the activities of the day. The players in each scene are different and use different scripts: for example, in interactions with friends in the neighborhood, with a stranger at the mall, or at Thanksgiving dinner with Grandma. Children must be able to subtly shift and adapt their behavior according to these varying contexts. As children develop, they demonstrate diverse competencies in these different scenes; with maturity, they learn to flow with ease from one scene to the next so that the play is successful.

There is an important developmental component that warrants consideration. Social behaviors follow a developmental continuum, just as other domains such as motor and cognitive development. Therefore, the social skills of a child at age 6 are considered primitive and out of place in a child age 11. There is also a dynamic interplay between social and play development. Parents may not focus as much attention on these domains as on the domains of speech acquisition or academic performance. Because of this, some children may develop major delays in social development before proper attention is paid to them.

We make a distinction between social skills and social competence (Schumaker & Hazel, 1984) for the purposes of this book. Social skills are defined as the cognitive functions and overt behaviors performed while interacting with others. Cognitive functions occur within the mind and are not visible, such as selective attention, organization, and memory, and include such capacities as understanding another person's feelings (empathy), making inferences about social cues, and evaluating the consequences of one's social conduct. Overt behaviors that illustrate social skills include the verbal and nonverbal actions that can be observed in conversations.

To further illustrate this definition of social skills, picture a water fountain in the hallway at a school. Three children are huddled around it in deep conversation, and a fourth child, a boy, is approaching them with an interest in entering the dialogue. The approaching child must perform a series of cognitive functions; he must determine who the other children are, the nature of their conversation, their readiness to include him, and how to join their discussion. After the instantaneous processing of this information, if the child decides that his presence would be welcome in the group, he will perform certain overt behaviors such as stepping up to the group in the right place, greeting the individuals, and contributing to the ongoing conversation. Alternatively, the child may make a judgment based on his cognitive functions that the other children would not welcome him into this gathering, and his subsequent overt behavior would be to continue walking down the hall.

Social competence as used in this book is an evaluative term based on judgments of the adequacy of the individual's social performance and includes the use of a range of cognitive and overt social skills that produce positive consequences for the individual and for those with whom he or she interacts. Social skills can be considered discrete, learned mental operations and observable behaviors. Social competence is the integration and application of these social skills in a smoothly flowing sequence appropriate to the cultural context. In our approach there are five components that serve as the foundation for social competence: play and social behavior, self-regulation, communication, prosocial skills, and social decision making.

The quest for personal social competence is unrelenting during the school-age years. Most children are preoccupied by the desire to fit in, look good, and earn the respect of their peers. They highly prize being popular and having friends and live in perpetual fear of making a mistake that would humiliate them grievously. Much energy is invested in evading embarrassment and avoiding the loss of peers' respect. Social competence affects self-definition, self-esteem, and self-confidence, and is likewise influenced by those qualities. Through his or her social experiences, the child rehearses for the varied roles and interactions of adulthood.

Problems in Social Competence

Deficits in social competence can be understood in three categories (Gresham, 1998; Gresham & Elliott, 1990). First, the child may not have the cognitive, communicative, or motor strategies needed to succeed in social exchanges. Second, the child may have the prerequisite skills, but does not apply them in every day situations. This problem may be due to various factors such as poor motivation or the inability to generalize skills across situations. Third, the child may have poor self-control and display aversive social behaviors. These three deficit areas are not incompatible and may be interrelated in some children. These deficits make children less socially effective, and therefore undermine their social status.

Poor social status with peers may be demonstrated by active rejection or neglect. Rejected children tend to be disruptive and aggressive, displaying little cooperative behavior. In contrast, children neglected by peers tend to be fearful and withdrawn and show little social initiation. A relatively strong correlation exists between poor peer relations in middle childhood and later school maladjustment, underachievement, dropping out of school during adolescence, juvenile delinquency, and adult crime. Likewise, children with poor social competence exhibit a disproportionate propensity toward mental health problems in later life (Elksnin & Elksnin, 1998; Kupersmidt, Coie, & Dodge, 1990; Walker, Colvin, & Ramsey, 1995).

Children with learning and developmental disabilities often display inadequate social performance (Kavale & Forness, 1996). Limitations in the following representative social skills appear to be predictive of poor peer acceptance:

- greeting and complimenting others;
- giving and accepting negative feedback;
- asking for, and providing, information;
- extending an offer of inclusion;
- negotiating situations involving conflict; and
- effective leave taking.

Research studies have consistently reported that, as a group, children with learning disabilities are less well-liked and more often rejected or ignored by peers (Gresham & MacMillan, 1997; LaGreca & Stone, 1990). These children have the lowest frequency of participation in school activities and are less likely to be involved in community-based activities such as clubs. Their poor interpersonal relations with siblings, teachers, parents, and other adults have also been documented.

Children with developmental and learning disabilities often have difficulties in self-regulation, communication, and social decision making. Difficulties in self-regulation seem to undermine the ability to pay attention and stay engaged in tasks; children in this group frequently display poor eye contact, hyperactivity, and behavioral excesses. In the communicative domain, many of these children are not skilled in initiating and maintaining conversation, have difficulty in eliciting positive responses from peers and teachers, are less cooperative during peer interaction, and have less informative and persuasive discourse than conversational partners. Such children often display fewer positive social behaviors and are more prone to negative peer interactions.

In addition, some children with disabilities have limited social decision-making skills. They may be less sensitive to nonverbal cues that convey the affect and intentions of others and have a restricted appreciation of the social nuances that support the formation of friendships. Overall, the ultimate psychological adjustment of children with social deficits is influenced more heavily by their social problems than by their academic difficulties. This impaired social behavior tends to persist over time and appears to be associated in adulthood with poor psychological well-being and underemployment.

In summary, the social inadequacy of many children with disabilities is a major concern that warrants direct intervention. Research shows that many children with disabilities do not model the behavior of non-disabled peers merely as a result of exposure to them (Hull, Venn, Lee, & Van Buren, 2000). Therefore regular education placement is not a guarantee of social acceptance. For inclusion to accomplish this objective, knowledgeable practitioners and parents must address the child's social competencies in a formal and deliberate way.

Common Intervention Approaches

Currently there is an expanding interest in helping children, both with and without disabilities, develop greater proficiency in the social arena. Tools on the market range from popular press how-to books for parents to advanced curricular designs for formal school settings. Researchers are clarifying the nature of the social difficulties, and there is an increasing awareness of the need for efficacy studies regarding the impact of intervention.

Historically there have been four primary reasons for hesitancy in addressing social skills in the classroom. Some educators feel that teaching social skills limits time for the academic program, while others feel that social-skills training is the responsibility of the family. Some consider social skills to be a reflection of the child's personality and not behaviors amenable to direct instruction, while many teachers feel ill-prepared to address social skills as a curricular concern. Fortunately, there is a shift in attitudes regarding the social needs of children as well as a growing awareness that social abilities can be enhanced through intervention. Educational materials and resources have been developed to support professional practice. Currently, the most frequently used intervention models are the instructional and social problem-solving approaches.

Instructional Approach

The instructional approach is the most commonly used method to promote social skills and is typically employed in school settings where commercially available curricula are used to teach a list of skills. Most of these programs are designed for children in regular education; a few of the curricula focus on children with disabilities. Depending upon the particular curriculum, the program may emphasize increasing prosocial skills, decreasing problem behaviors, fostering peer acceptance, and successful inclusion of children with special needs.

Typically, these programs specify the skills or desired social behaviors that are the objectives to be taught. A list might include managing teasing, taking turns talking, giving criticism constructively, controlling aggressive impulses, and following rules when playing games. There is a lesson plan for each skill to be taught. The standard format is to begin with a statement of the behavioral objective to be addressed that includes a definition of the social skill.

Next, the adult demonstrates the skill by modeling the behavior. This step is followed by time for the children to practice the new behavior either in a role-play or group exercise. The lesson plan is completed with feedback and discussion about the children's performance. Most of the curricula using an instructional approach are designed for implementation in school and focus on enhancing the social behaviors necessary for classroom success.

The instructional approach has many disadvantages (Gresham, 1998; Rutherford, 1997; Zaragoza, Vaughn, & McIntosh, 1991). The curricula predominantly address classroom-related behaviors, and these may not be the same skills that are valued by classmates and promote peer social acceptance. There are real differences between the social demands of the classroom and the friendship-building demands of peer interaction. Another disadvantage is the restricted ability to generalize these skills across a wide variety of situations. Children have difficulty generalizing their classroom-acquired social skills to the informal, unstructured encounters often found in the playground, neighborhood, and home. Also, the focus of these curricula is generally on the performance of the class as a group and not on the specific needs of individual children; the lack of personalized intervention is a major drawback. Given the complexity of the social difficulties of many children, goals and intervention strategies are most effective when tailored to the presenting needs of each child (see Table 1.1).

Table 1.1
Features of the Instructional and Social Problem-Solving Approaches

Focus on skill acquisition or the reasoning process

Didactic instruction

Predetermined, group-oriented curriculum

Coping predominantly with the classroom

Practice exercises

Limited generalization

Do not emphasize friendship building

Not personalized

This point is made in the case of Derek. During a lesson on sharing information, Derek had demonstrated adequate skill. Later that day, Derek had an opportunity to apply this skill when he was telling his friend Steven how to complete a joint class assignment. Steven was inattentive, and Derek displayed two inappropriate responses. First, he was bossy and demanded Steven's immediate participation; when this failed, Derek withdrew in a sullen mood. In this spontaneous interaction, there was a breakdown in Derek's social performance due in part to his lack of perspective taking combined with poor reading of nonverbal cues. Derek failed to consider Steven's viewpoint; Steven may have been tired, interested in doing something else, or unenthusiastic about the assignment. In this social context Derek was unsuccessful and could not generalize his learning. The teacher's original lesson did not individualize instruction to address Derek's poor reading of nonverbal cues and inadequate perspective taking. Instead, she taught a generic lesson on sharing information with others that Derek was unable to generalize to a new context.

Social Problem-Solving Approach

The social problem-solving approach, which teaches skills in decision making and problem solving, is a multistep process that includes noticing and accurately interpreting social clues, generating possible solutions to the social situation, evaluating the efficacy of each solution, choosing and implementing a choice, and evaluating the result. Children with special needs may have difficulty with any one or a combination of these steps. Curricula using this approach generally provide structured lessons that teach each of the steps in sequence. Although each cognitive step of the process may be taught individually, an emphasis is placed on integrating all the steps into a functional whole. Whereas an instructional approach teaches discrete prosocial skills, the social problem-solving approach teaches a way of reasoning. With age, a child's number and quality of decision-making strategies increases. For example, the ability to generate alternative solutions is rather limited in the preschool child, but by adolescence the child should have sophisticated cause and effect thinking and be able to articulate required steps to solve a social problem (see Table 1.1).

Social problem-solving interventions tend to increase the problem-solving skills of children but have little impact on their social behavior in everyday naturalistic environments (Beelman, Pfingsten, & Losel, 1994). Because improvements in social decision making do not necessarily result in enhanced social competence per se, social problem-solving intervention must be integrated into a functional context.

In general, programs using the instructional and/or social problem-solving approaches do not show the ability to produce large, important changes in the social behavior of children with or without disabilities (Gresham, Sugai, & Horner, 2001; Quinn, Kavale, Mathur, Rutherford, & Forness, 1999). Meta-analytic studies show that traditional social-skills training has only modest effects; these limited results are related to the previously mentioned disadvantages of the two approaches. The focus on isolated skill training is artificial and not supportive of generalization to other environments (Haring, 1992; Sheridan, Hungelmann, & Maughan, 1999), making the use of contrived lessons that are taught in decontextualized group settings of particular concern. Rather, the most effective intervention is the one that incorporates elements from the real world. There is a trend toward teaching social skills in naturalistic settings using informal procedures based on incidental learning (Gresham, 1998) and a movement from traditional social skills training to coaching the children throughout the school day.

In our activity-based approach the focus is on children engaged in social interaction within the context of authentic play and leisure pursuits, whether in social competence groups or in daily routines. The emphasis is on building the competencies necessary for making and sustaining friendships rather than acquiring isolated social skills.

The Activity-Based Approach

Engagement in physical and social activity is the core of our intervention frame of reference. Developmental and cognitive growth are mediated by the emotional experiences of children involved in play and daily routines, and intense emotional feelings are associated with attempts to learn about and master the child's world. Affect drives learning, and learning fuels affect. The development of a complex social repertoire is acquired through interpersonal transactions with peers and adults. Successful engagement in activity promotes confidence, self-esteem, and an "I can" mindset. When there is a history of social failure, children acquire the opposite expectation. The therapeutic aim is to provide an *experiential laboratory* in which the child can manage developmentally appropriate social challenges, which may evolve from initially playing with objects to acquire prerequisite skills, to parallel play with one or two other children, to cooperative play with peers.

Our activity-based intervention approach is supported by a conceptual framework that addresses the complexity of social behavior, including purpose of interaction, perspective taking, and the five components of social competence. This orientation emphasizes the therapeutic use of peer interaction while engaged in naturalistic, age-appropriate activities. Play and leisure pursuits serve as the primary vehicles for intervention, and in the process the children expand their play and prosocial development. The selection, grading, and implementation of activities by the practitioner are critical to the success of this approach. The adult essentially serves as a coach who facilitates the interplay between the children as they acquire more sophisticated interpersonal skills.

The instructional and social problem-solving approaches need to be expanded into a more functional and integrated orientation (see Table 1.2). Social learning occurs along a continuum from incidental to formal. Children learn social skills in the context of moment-to-moment daily living: in episodes at the dining room table; with the cashier in the supermarket; during daily exchanges at the bus stop; with teammates at soccer practice; hanging out at the swimming pool; and through cooperative learning tasks in school. Some social behaviors are directly taught by adults, for example, the culturally relevant behaviors for family gatherings. Other social skills are learned more indirectly as children watch and imitate the behavior of others. For instance, children may learn to play cooperatively on the jungle gym by imitating the turn taking of other children, or children may learn to repair disagreements by observing their parents having a squabble and making up.

Table 1.2
Features of the Activity-Based Approach

Focus on learning within play and leisure activities

Coaching and modeling

Flexible, personalized plan

Coping with school, home, and community

Practice in naturalistic, interpersonal contexts

Addresses social behaviors plus prerequisite skills

Rich, frequent opportunities for spontaneous learning & practice

Promotes generalization

Emphasizes building friendships

Comprehensive conceptual framework

Ideally, children are able to acquire social competence through direct teaching and incidental learning. Our activity-based approach blends both of these methods to maximize the potential for learning and avoid the common limitation of focusing solely on teaching structured concrete lessons that have minimum carryover into the daily environments of the child. Our approach attempts to approximate normal learning experiences by integrating teaching techniques and varied play opportunities within the context of the child's involvement in naturalistic activities and social interactions.

The contrast between the different intervention approaches can be seen in the example of learning the prosocial skill of greeting others. Many young children tend to omit greetings in their enthusiasm to talk about what is on their mind, but the activity of greeting others becomes increasingly significant in peer relations during adolescence. The nature, timing, and cultural expression of greeting behaviors are critical, and the greeting of a first grader is quite different from the greeting of a seventh grader or a 12th grader. A child needs to know whether "Hey, what's up!" and the high five sign are current, out of vogue, or do not fit the group at hand.

A standard instructional approach would introduce the topic and its importance, then two people would model ways to greet one another, followed by pairs of children role-playing greeting each other in front of the class; the observing children and adults would then provide feedback regarding the performance. This instructional approach typically falls short of preparing the child for the dynamic, culturally determined nature of greeting behaviors. The curriculum may provide scripts that the children memorize through rehearsal and include generic greetings such as "Hello, how are you?" and "What's your name?"; but such a static approach, so far removed from the realities of daily discourse, is not very functional.

Our activity-based approach may begin with an informal and personal account of the importance of greeting, such as "It makes me feel good when friends greet me because it shows that they are glad to see me." The conversation could continue with questions and discussion about different types of greetings. The adult would demonstrate the greetings most relevant to the group members, including the differences in greeting various people such as grandparents, other adults, peers, and strangers. Group members then would be invited to practice personalized greetings. To motivate the group members to practice greeting spontaneously in everyday encounters, a secret greeting could be chosen for temporary use; this greeting would be used with conspiratorial delight whenever approaching fellow group members. In addition to this intervention, a play activity could be designed that encourages the use of greeting behaviors in an impromptu and natural way; for example, children could play knights at a castle in which there is frequent coming and going that requires the use of greetings to gain entry.

There are four major characteristics of an activity-based approach to the development of social competence (see Table 1.3).

Table 1.3
Characteristics of an Activity-Based Approach

Activity-based play and leisure pursuits

Multidimensional conceptual framework

Linked to the child's major social contexts

Appropriate for a wide variety of children

1. **Activity-based play and leisure pursuits serve as the primary vehicles for intervention.** The child's direct involvement in age-appropriate, enticing activity is the most powerful way of learning the foundations of social competence. Participation in highly valued, child-oriented activities serves as the primary experience upon which intervention is grounded and elicits the child's interactive behavior and affect. Through experiential learning during play, the child practices the desired social skills. In part, the role of the practitioner is to coach the child in ways to interact while engaged in play and leisure activities; in this way, the intervention proceeds along a natural course while behavior is being modified.

2. **Intervention is based on a multidimensional conceptual framework.** Social competence is a balance of many complex parts, each of which contributes uniquely to the child's overall social ability. Consequently, intervention must go beyond the consideration of isolated social skills to a broad view of interrelated and integrated elements. Our intervention approach has three dimensions. First, there is a concern for the purpose of social interaction; second, the model examines the development of a world view or perspective taking; and third, the components of social competence are emphasized, including social and play behavior, self-regulation, communication, prosocial skills, and social decision making.

3. **Intervention is linked to the child's major social contexts of home, school, and community.** Each social context has a cultural expectation for behavior; for example, expected behavior at the physician's office is different from that at the soccer field or a wedding. As a result, behavior is deemed adequate or inadequate based on the demands of the social context. Due to the power of context as an influence, intervention seeks to create an environmental setting that supports effective interactions. For example, the practitioner may work with the bus driver or parent to modify elements of the environment that elicit a child's aggressive behavior, or the practitioner may simulate a particular social context within a group therapy setting such as snack time to simulate the school lunch.

4. **This approach is designed to address the needs of a wide variety of children.** Appropriate for children from preschool to age 12, our approach will benefit children with a wide variety of disabilities as well as children who are developing on target except for their social skills. It will also enrich the experiences of children participating in regular sports and recreational programs.

Our approach targets not only desired prosocial behavior but also the child's underlying difficulties that are interfering with his or her social learning. Activities are chosen to address such problems as inattention, anxiety, and poor pragmatic skills. At the same time, our approach facilitates social and play development.

There are many ways to apply this activity-based approach.

- Components of this model can be incorporated in the provision of one-to-one therapy; for example, as a speech-language pathologist is working on articulation, socially relevant pragmatic skills can be emphasized.

- When acting as a consultant in a school or a community-based agency, the practitioner can provide guidance regarding the social needs of the children and ways to address them in the context of the program. For instance, an occupational therapist can make recommendations to summer camp personnel on behalf of a specific child about strategies for strengthening his or her emerging cooperative play.

- A particularly effective strategy is to conduct social competence groups for children with social skills difficulties; these groups can be conducted in a school, a clinic, a neighborhood program, or a private practice.

- Some practitioners may run therapeutic groups with a variety of purposes, taking advantage of the group setting and add a social component to it. Examples include adding a social focus to a handwriting, fine motor, or language acquisition group.

Table 1.4 presents sample applications in a variety of contexts.

Table 1.4
Applications of an Activity-Based Approach in a Variety of Contexts

Consultant

Diverse therapeutic groups

Community-based programs

Social competence groups

One-to-one therapy

Foundations of Social Behavior

Mature social behavior involves a person's ability to understand the viewpoints, thoughts, and feelings of his- or herself and others, and the ability to act on this understanding. It is based on the infant's innate capacities for relating as well as experiences from parent-child interaction. These factors help to establish attachment between the primary caregivers and the young child, and early social development emerges in this context. Social behavior is intimately intertwined with interactive play, which can be as fundamental as peek-a-boo between parent and infant or as elaborate as player interactions in the game *Dungeons and Dragons*™.

Play is a critical activity for learning and self-expression, providing opportunities for the child to organize thoughts, feelings, and skills within the context of discovering the new and making sense of the familiar. Play, which integrates the child's internal and external worlds, is a spontaneous, voluntary involvement that is initiated and regulated by the child. The acts of play are performed for their own intrinsic reward. Because the child is in command, the constraints of reality can be ignored for free expression of emotions, fantasy, and imagination. Problems in social and play behavior do not appear spontaneously at any given age. Often, there are discernible difficulties in interpersonal relations and play in the first years of life.

This section discusses the early beginnings and development of social behavior and play behavior. First, the social capacities of infants that form the foundation for later social skill acquisition are examined. Next, temperament is described as a particularly critical personality variable that shapes the child's social behavior from the start. These constitutional factors influence the child's development of attachment, as well as the parent-child interaction that is the major arena for acquiring early social competencies. A practitioner working with a child will benefit from knowing if the presenting social problems are related to a long-standing history of insecure attachment or are of more recent development.

Capacities of the Infant That Support Relationships

Infants have amazing capacities for processing information from the physical and social environment, discriminating among various parts of the environment, and developing expectations or predictions about how the environment will function. Infants are neurobiologically prepared for social relationships from birth; they have constitutionally based capacities for seeking out and preferring their primary caregivers. A child learns to modulate emotions and develops a sense of self through the process of relating to others. The following emerging capacities of infants contribute to the early recognition and preference for the caregiver: the ability to engage in mutual, reciprocal communication; the development of expectations for interactions; and the emotional availability of each partner.

- In the first week, an infant can discriminate the smell of its own mother's milk.

- Within the first week, an infant has a preference for its mother's native language over any other language. During fetal life the child becomes accustomed to the melody, stress, and timing of the mother's speech pattern.

- By 1 month of age, an infant can differentiate between its mother's voice and another woman's voice.

- By 1 month of age, an infant can differentiate between the features of its mother's face and those of another woman.

- By 3 months of age, an infant can adapt differentially to the mother and father in terms of the kind of anticipatory and reciprocal movements that each evokes, and can even respond to the sound of each voice with movements uniquely adapted to the particular parent.

- By 5 to 6 months of age, an infant can make use of social referencing, intensely studying the familiar adult for clues as to how a situation should be interpreted: for example, using the father's facial expression as a clue whether to be wary or comfortable with a loud stranger.

Temperament

Although temperament is defined in differing ways, most definitions reflect some variation of the definition originally postulated by Allport (1937):

> Temperament refers to the characteristic phenomena of an individual's emotional nature, including his susceptibility to emotional stimulation, his customary strength and speed of response, the quality of his prevailing mood, and all the peculiarities of fluctuation and intensity of mood; these phenomena being regarded as dependent upon constitutional make-up, and therefore largely hereditary in origin. (p. 54)

There is general agreement that temperament is evidenced in behavioral tendencies rather than in specific, discrete behaviors. Theorists emphasize temperament's biological base and acknowledge the relative continuity of these behavioral tendencies over time, while recognizing that the expression of temperamental attributes is shaped and modified as a consequence of experience. The impact of temperament is most direct and evident in infancy when idiosyncratic coping styles are developing. In the view of Rothbart and Derryberry (1981), temperament refers to constitutionally based differences in reactivity and self-regulation, with reactivity defined as the biological sensitivity of the individual's response to changes in the environment. Self-regulation involves the attention and behavioral patterns of approach and avoidance that are used to modulate this reactivity.

The work of Thomas and Chess (1977) deserves special note because of its influence on the study of temperament and its use in clinical practice. Temperament is conceptualized as the stylistic component of behavior, as patterns in how actions are performed in contrast to the motivation and content of behavior. Thomas and Chess describe the following nine dimensions of temperament. Although these dimensions are not definitive, they provide a useful frame of reference when considering a young child's temperament.

- Rhythmicity, or regularity of body functions, including hunger, excretion, sleep, and wakefulness

- Approach/withdrawal in response to new situations

- Adaptability to new or changed situations

- Threshold of responsiveness, or amount of stimulation required to elicit a response

- General activity level (i.e., high, medium, variable, low)

- Intensity, or strength of reactions

- Distractibility, or the degree to which extraneous stimuli alter behavior

- Attention span and persistence, or the amount of time devoted to an activity and diligence in the face of obstacles or interference

- Quality of mood, or the amount of pleasant, friendly, joyful behavior as contrasted with unpleasant, unfriendly, unhappy behavior

In addition, Thomas and Chess describe three behavioral clusters, designated respectively as easy, difficult, and slow-to-warm-up temperaments, while emphasizing that a substantial percentage of infants do not neatly fall into any one of the three.

Easy or flexible children are rhythmic, positive in initial approach, adaptive, mild in intensity, and positive in mood. Regular in their habits, these children respond positively to new situations, adapt quickly to new foods and people, and are generally cheerful; they enjoy learning new games and taking part in new activities.

Difficult or feisty infants are irregular in rhythm, negative in approach and tending to withdraw, slow to adapt, intense, and negative in mood. These children display great irregularity in eating, sleeping, and eliminating. They tend to withdraw noisily or protest vigorously when exposed to any new stimulus or situation such as unfamiliar food, clothing, people, or places. Although eventually they adapt, initial exposure to new demands, such as going to a nursery school or a birthday party, typically elicit howling or other negative behavior from these children.

Slow-to-warm-up or fearful infants are low in activity, negative in approach, slow to adapt, mild in intensity, and negative in mood. They adapt cautiously and tend to withdraw from new situations but with little or no fussing. As infants, these children are likely to respond to a new food by letting it dribble out of their mouths; in nursery school, they stay on the sidelines for several weeks; in kindergarten, if pushed to take part in some new activity, they struggle quietly to escape.

Thomas and Chess (1977) derived these dimensions and styles of temperament from an investigation of a small number of children who initially participated in their longitudinal study, and this seminal effort generated research that examined the study's results. In general, the nine dimensions of temperament do not emerge in factor-analytic studies using scales designed to measure the dimensions. There is some consensus in the field that salient variables of temperament are fewer than nine in number and are related to activity, reactivity, emotionality, and sociability (Goldsmith et al., 1987).

The relationship between temperament and social competence is complex and not well understood; however, temperament may influence social competence in at least four ways. First, temperament may influence the child's exposure to potentially stressful situations. For example, a child with a high activity level may explore the environment vigorously and therefore be confronted with a greater number of potential stressors. Second, temperament may determine the child's range of sensitivity to stress; a child with strong sensory reactivity and arousal may have a low tolerance to environmental stimulation before becoming distressed. Third, temperament may influence the characteristic pattern of the child's social behavior, possibly modulating the latency, duration, and intensity of the child's behavioral responses and emotional expression. Fourth, temperament may affect the willingness of parents and others to be available to the child, as certain temperamental attributes tend to evoke social support and nurturing parental practices, while others foster rejection (Zeitlin & Williamson, 1994).

Temperament contributes to the child's constitutional responsiveness to the environment as well as self-regulation. For instance, temperament may affect the ability to cope with an unfamiliar social situation by influencing the degree of sensitivity and susceptibility of the child to new stimuli. It may also shape the timing and intensity of the child's behavior, such as the latency and vigor of reaching out or moving away. An appreciation of the child's temperamental attributes enables parents and practitioners to modify the child's behavior to encourage adaptive functioning. For example, an adult dealing with a child with a feisty temperament can establish an orderly routine of daily activities but follow the schedule in a flexible manner. The adult can also avoid environmental overstimulation and offer the opportunity for vigorous play in order for the child to discharge physical energy. Thus, children with feisty temperaments may be socially successful if adults are responsive to their needs.

Parent-Child Interaction

During the early months of life, an infant and its parents get to know each other and learn to communicate. During this time of getting acquainted, both parties are practicing how to express needs, understand the actions of others, and modulate emotional expressions. This mutually reciprocal, two-way communication forms the basis for relating and is the foundation for interactive behavior in childhood (see Table 2.1).

Table 2.1
Parent-Child Interaction

Sample Parent Contributions	Sample Infant Contributions
Visual attention	Alert/interest
Emotional tone	Child initiated social behavior
Expands behavior of child	Aware of parent's emotional state
Mirrors child's feeling state	Assertive/persistent/impulsive
Responsive to cues	Exploratory play
Responds to distress	Consolability
	Emerging self-regulation

The following dialogue between a father and his 4-month-old baby illustrates this point. The father sends messages to the child by exaggerating his facial expression, playing with the pitch of his voice, speaking "parentese," and looming his head close to the baby, then pulling back. These behaviors typically cause the baby to become excited. However, the infant must be able to control the intensity of this interaction in order to maintain self-control and prevent sensory overload. There are a number of strategies a baby can use to reduce tension, such as turning the head away, averting the eyes, changing facial expression, and yawning. A dramatic "dance" between the father and child occurs, in which each take turns leading the interaction as well as adjusting the tempo and intensity of the exchange. A rhythm is noted in this back and forth pattern that is punctuated by frequent mismatches and repairs.

The parent and infant each make significant contributions to this interactive dance (Clark, 1985; Clark, Paulson, & Conlin, 1993; Kelly & Barnard, 2000). Parents are particularly responsible for monitoring the visual attention and emotional tone of the pair; they mirror the infant's feeling state and respond to cues and distress. Parents also help the infant expand and elaborate emerging behavior. For instance, Maria notices that baby Jennifer is thrashing her arms vigorously and looking in one direction. The mother searches around to find the object of Jennifer's interest and sees the family cat, Toby, who is sneaking into the room. Maria responds in a tone that matches Jennifer's gleeful excitement, calling out, "Here Kitty! Here Kitty! Come here!" Jennifer begins to vocalize, almost perfectly matching the quality of her mother's voice.

Infants also make an important contribution to the parent-child interaction, demonstrating a level of alertness and interest that influences engagement. Infants are aware of the parent's emotional state and initiate social behavior; they also contribute exploratory play that invites interaction. The emerging capacity for self-regulation influences interactions, including the ability to be consoled by another. Infants vary in their degree of assertiveness, persistence, and impulsivity; likewise, their activity level influences the quality of the parent-child inter-action. During bath time, 10-month-old Sammy and his father illustrate the infant's contribution to their interaction. Sammy is robust and active, splashing the water in the tub. When water splashes into his father's face, Daddy responds with a startled look and laughter, to which Sammy reacts by initiating more vigorous splashing. This leads to a water fight with Daddy; Sammy sustains the splashing in an assertive, persistent manner until his father calls a truce. Through this type of social engagement, young children learn ways of communicating and relating.

Attachment

Attachment is a long-lasting relationship characterized by a strong emotional bond between two individuals. The first and essential attachment relationship is between the infant and the mother or another significant caregiver. A child actively seeks closeness to its attachment figure, particularly at times of stress. Attachment patterns are active throughout life as people establish deep emotional connections to new significant individuals.

There are at least three reasons why the topic of attachment is relevant to the discussion of social competence. First, the infant initially experiences the feelings of relating through attachments. These interpersonal emotions are influenced by two kinds of needs, the satisfaction of physical survival needs such as hunger and discomfort, and the satisfaction of social emotional needs such as the expression of pleasure or frustration. Second, attachments provide the opportunity to learn the rules of interaction, as discussed earlier. Third, through the attachment experience the infant develops expectations and beliefs about the nature of social engagement. Examples of these pre-linguistic, emotionally based beliefs include the development of trust, the desirability of being in relationships, the hierarchy of attachments by importance, and emerging expectations of success and failure. A child's early attachments have an enduring influence on social development and the capacity for acquiring and maintaining friendships.

The two primary patterns of attachment in young children are secure and insecure attachment. The insecure pattern is further divided into avoidant, ambivalent, and disorganized/disoriented patterns (Zeanah, Mammen, & Leiberman, 1993).

- **Secure Pattern** — Infants with secure attachments have warm, loving relationships with the attachment figure and use that individual as a secure base from which to explore the surroundings. Approximately 60% to 65% of infants can be considered securely attached. Typically, these children have accessible and responsive caregivers. By kindergarten age these children are generally more cooperative, sociable, competent, and ego-resilient than children in the insecure attachment category. The children tend to be persistent and enthusiastic in the way they manage cognitive tasks and are generally preferred by peers and teachers to children with insecure attachments.

- **Avoidant Pattern** — Infants with avoidant attachments are covertly anxious about the availability of the attachment figure and have developed a defensive posture for managing their anxiety. About 20% of infants are classified in this category. Avoidant attachments may be fostered by angry and rejecting parents or by prolonged unresponsiveness such as in situations of neglect. As they get older, the behavior of these children is often seen as detached and restricted in emotional awareness; they have difficulty in expressing negative emotions and do not acknowledge normal imperfections. Because they do not believe that other people will respond favorably toward them, these children do not request practical help and emotional support. Avoidant children frequently have limited fantasy play and tend to focus instead on concrete object play.

- **Ambivalent Pattern** — Anxiety and mixed feelings about the attachment figure are readily seen in infants with ambivalent attachments. Approximately 10% of infants are classified as ambivalent. An erratic and unpredictable pattern of caregiving tends to produce ambivalent attachments. These children tend to be less enthusiastic, compliant, and persistent than securely attached children; they also tend to express more anger and frustration. Ambivalently attached children demonstrate inconsistent behavior that facilitates mixed and sometimes hostile responses from peers; as a result, their ambivalent feelings about others are further reinforced.

- **Disorganized/Disoriented Pattern** — These infants do not have consistent strategies for managing separation and reunion with the attachment figure. They present in diverse ways including deep disturbance or depression, severe disorganization, and a mixed pattern of avoidance, anger, and attachment. An estimated 10% to 15% of infants can be included in this category. These children are at risk for exhibiting hostile and aggressive behavior by 5 years of age. The picture of these children is tentative and incomplete because this category is only recently described in the literature and is the least understood.

The major determinant of an infant's attachment pattern is the quality of the parent's sensitivity in responding to the baby's needs and signals (Cassidy, 1997). The parent is, therefore, more instrumental in determining the nature of the attachment than the infant. Sensitive caregiving tends to produce secure attachments, whereas insensitive parental responsiveness fosters anxious attachment.

There are a number of risk factors that can place the relationship in jeopardy. Chronic irritability strains parent-child interactions and may lead to an anxious attachment; similarly, clinical depression in the parent undermines attachment. Limited social support for the parent reflects an absence of practical or emotional aid, and unstable or conflicted family contexts are also not conducive to secure attachments. The presence of one risk factor may not be sufficiently influential to shape the attachment pattern; however, two or more risk factors markedly increase the likelihood of the emergence of an insecure attachment. The frequencies of secure, avoidant, and ambivalent attachments are not significantly influenced by socio-economic status.

It is important clinically to gather attachment-related information when planning intervention to promote social competence. Care needs to be taken to ensure that information related to attachment is dealt with in a confidential and sensitive manner. This delicate material is gathered over time in a naturalistic way through observation and discussion, typically unfolding as trust between the parents and practitioner develops.

There are at least three reasons to address attachment issues during assessment and intervention. First and foremost, the attachment pattern of the child is clinically relevant because it influences social behavior and development. Also, there is a connection between the child's early attachment and later social competence. For example, infants who are securely attached at 1 year of age tend to be more outgoing, self-confident, interactive, and cooperative than children who were anxiously attached at that age, and as a result are generally better liked by peers and adults.

Second, gathering attachment-related information during the assessment process contributes to a greater understanding of the child's social and emotional strengths and vulnerabilities. Knowing the nature and evolution of the attachment pattern helps the practitioner to construct a profile of the child's current social behaviors (how the child behaves and why). For example, a child with an unstable family history devoid of intimacy and a sense of trust may find it very difficult to develop close, warm relationships with peers and the teacher. In a different scenario, a child with an emotionally impoverished family background may compensate by becoming overly attached to adults and demonstrate little interest in establishing friendships with peers.

Third, an awareness of the attachment history helps the practitioner when establishing goals and expectations for intervention. A history of an unhealthy parent-child relationship may indicate a need for particularly strong parent involvement in program planning and intervention and may also assist in clarifying how deep-seated the social problems may be. For instance, the practitioner would draw a different conclusion if social difficulties had recently appeared following placement in a new classroom rather than being the result of a longstanding series of failed group experiences going back to early childhood.

Knowing about attachment-related issues when beginning an alliance with a family is extremely useful. The following vignette is an example of this strategy in use.

Manuel is a 5-year-old boy whose parents referred him to a private therapy practice due to social rejection by his peers. As a result of an initial assessment, Manuel was placed in a social competence group that met on a weekly basis. Over time, the ambivalence and insecurity of the mother-child relationship became apparent; beginning with the first session, the mother was panicky when she had to separate from her son and the boy was highly resistant to joining the group. For instance, he persisted in taking two rubber dragons with him into the sessions, despite the mother's reminders to leave them in his backpack. Eventually the mother reported that she has always had anxious feelings about her son because he has a difficult temperament and personality and was erratic in his behavior, varying from clinging, demanding, and angry to affectionate and charming.

This knowledge about the attachment pattern between Manuel and his mother helped the practitioner to determine the best approach for establishing a therapeutic alliance. Due to this insecure, ambivalent attachment, the therapist felt it was important not to place the parent and child under additional stress but rather to employ a slow, gentle, and under-standing approach. Essentially, the goal was the same for both child and parent: the practitioner wanted to help them to adapt to the therapeutic setting and feel comfortable, and their anxiety needed to be reduced to help enable them to change.

The therapist used two strategies to address this goal with the mother. First, the therapist assured her that Manuel was quickly becoming accepted in the group; this information decreased her ambivalence and worry that her son might be having another failure with peers. In addition, the therapist provided guidance and support regarding techniques that would assist the mother in managing particular behaviors such as outbursts of anger and clinging behavior. The therapist validated the mother's feelings by recognizing that Manuel was a child who would challenge any parent's patience and skills.

The therapeutic alliance was nurtured with Manuel in a somewhat similar way. The priority from the start was to establish a bond between the boy and the therapist; this was accomplished when the therapist made Manuel feel welcome with an open invitation to participate in the group. No limits were set, other than those to protect property and the psychological and physical safety of the children, despite Manuel's testing behaviors. No coaching or demands for behavioral change were made until Manuel demonstrated trust of and attachment to the therapist.

As seen above, an understanding of the attachment pattern was instrumental in knowing how to facilitate a therapeutic relationship with Manuel and his mother. This strategy helps address social competence issues between the child and the caregiver, which helps to extend the strategy beyond the therapeutic setting.

Conceptual Framework

Type and Nature of Interactions

The elements of social competence are presented in the conceptual framework of our approach (see Figure 3.1). These elements include the purpose of interactions, the progression from egocentricity to social perspective taking, and the five components of social competence. This conceptual framework is designed to enhance the social performance of children ages 3 to 12 years who have inadequate interpersonal skills and is based primarily on a developmental perspective.

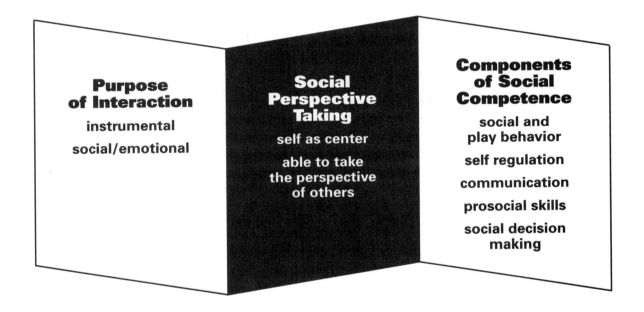

Figure 3.1
Foundations of Social Competence

This conceptual framework can be used in clinical practice with other complimentary frames of reference; for example, a cognitive-behavioral approach in teaching skills or a group dynamics approach in understanding peer relations. Likewise, this framework can be integrated with neurodevelopmental treatment, sensory integration, or language acquisition frameworks to add a social component to the interventions. As an example, a therapist working to enhance the motivation of children with motor planning difficulties may discover an advantage to working with a group of two or three children together. Thus activities with a focus on motor planning can be modified to include the collaboration with buddies in order to successfully complete the task.

The conceptual framework addresses the most common deficits of children that undermine their social performance: social and play behavior; self-regulation; communication; prosocial skills; and social decision making. Intervention is developmentally sequenced according to the functional levels of the children. A comprehensive repertoire of activities and therapeutic procedures is used to increase experiential learning and the generalization of social skills. In discussing the conceptual framework, this chapter addresses the purpose of interactions and social perspective taking. Chapter 4 focuses on social and play behavior, an important component of social competence. Chapter 5 completes the discussion of the conceptual framework by discussing the components of self-regulation, communication, prosocial skills, and social decision-making.

Purpose of Interactions

Social interactions can be thought of as the everyday conversations, encounters, and relationships people have with each other (Gutstein, 2000). As depicted in our conceptual framework, these interactions can be considered either instrumental or social-emotional in nature. Instrumental interactions serve the purpose of attaining a tangible end or concrete goal, such as achieving some type of material, physical, informational, or financial gain. These interactions emphasize performing tasks and achieving productive outcomes. Some examples are purchasing an item at a store, asking for directions for a bus trip, arranging a social event, or trading baseball cards. These types of interactions involve common types of discourse in the home, school, and neighborhood, such as:

"Finish your homework."

"Feed the dog."

"Are we there yet?"

"After lunch, let's play catch."

"Can Joanie sleep over this weekend?"

"Dad, my allowance is way too small!"

"Put your pencils down when you are finished."

Social-emotional interactions are designed to acquire and maintain more intimate friendships and family relationships. These interactions meet attachment needs by making acquaintances, engaging in social conversation, and sharing emotions and experiences. Often these transactions may include information, opinions, and feelings that deal with a variety of emotional expressions such as love, joy, hate, ambivalence, alienation, wishes, or preferences. These interactions are often used to help someone feel good and reflect acceptance, appreciation, and intimacy. Such interactions are implied in the capacity to shoot the breeze, chit chat, make small talk, and hang out.

Social-emotional interactions are seen in such contexts as striking up a conversation to pass the time, catching up with classroom gossip, sharing love between grandparents and grandchildren, and complaining about the teacher not being fair. Sample social-emotional exchanges include:

"Yo, what's up?"

"You make me laugh when you say that."

"I really hate her; she stole my boyfriend!"

"Oh Grandma, you smell so good."

"I'm sorry your puppy got killed by the car."

Both social-emotional and instrumental interactions can involve interpersonal communication of varying degrees of complexity, duration, and frequency. Some situations can be managed with a simple exchange of ideas or feelings, whereas others require extended and in-depth interactions. In general, social-emotional interactions tend to be less concrete, more abstract, and governed by more ambiguous rules. Therefore, children with social challenges often find social-emotional interactions more difficult than instrumental interactions. In fact, a common problem is that these children have few social-emotional interactions. Consequently, they try to use instrumental communication methods to meet social-emotional goals. Often the outcome is one of rejection, confusion, or irritation, as illustrated in the following scenes.

Jason wanted to make a social connection with T. J., but because Jason did not know how to make small talk, he used instrumental communication by focusing on T. J.'s binoculars. He tried to maintain a discussion by explaining how binoculars work until T. J. told him to get lost.

In another example, Buddy was with a group of children who were talking about a computer game. The chatter became lively as they discussed how scary the monsters were in this game. Buddy lost the flow of the discourse as it shifted to this social-emotional level, as he was stuck at the initial instrumental interaction regarding levels of achievement in the game. As he bragged about reaching level 6, the other children ignored him while they became increasingly engaged in their shared emotional experience.

Children should be able to shift between instrumental and social-emotional communication depending on the purpose of the interaction. Most children with social deficits have some capacity, albeit possibly limited, for both types of interaction. The practitioner needs to identify what interferes with the child's abilities to apply the two patterns appropriately and to shift flexibly between them. Difficulties in other components of the conceptual framework negatively influence this development, including the impact of impaired self-regulation and social decision-making on the ability to shift between instrumental and social-emotional interactions.

Social Perspective Taking

The conceptual framework also addresses social perspective taking. There is a developmental progression in the child's world view, developing from an early egotistical pattern of viewing the self as the center of the universe into the ability to take the perspective of others and attain a societal view. From a *me* orientation of self, children develop the capacity for empathy and moral judgment. They are increasingly able to de-center from their own motives, feelings, and perspectives to recognize those of others. In this process of socialization, children develop improved communication skills, the capacity for moral standards regarding the welfare of others, and the ability to engage in relationships based on mutual understanding.

Those working with children need to keep in mind the developmental sequence in this shift in role-taking ability (Selman & Jacquette, 1978). From the undifferentiated egocentric perspective of the preschool child, there is a progression to a more differentiated perspective around age 5; that is, from the initial inability to distinguish his or her own perspective from others, the child begins to realize that he or she and others may have the same or different perspectives. From ages 6 to 7 there are reciprocal perspectives, as children are able to see themselves from another's perspective and are aware that the other person can do the same thing. As a result, there is more give and take in social exchanges, as children consider the feelings of others.

By ages 9 to 10, children have acquired mutual perspectives and can distance themselves from both parties in a relationship and study it from a third person's perspective. During this stage, children begin to use this perspective-taking skill to enrich their relationships — becoming more intimate, supportive, and, at times, cliquey with their peers. An increasingly mature, societal perspective in role taking emerges around age 12. Children of this age have developed the capacity to see group perspectives such as the commonalities and differences within and between groups, such as a Little League team, the boys in a class, or Native Americans. This perspective facilitates the individual's moral and altruistic development as well as the possibility to reach deeper levels of intimacy within relationships.

A child may demonstrate delays in social perspective taking or exhibit temporary regressions under times of stress. Someone still functioning at an early egocentric level of development may have trouble determining what is done intentionally or unintentionally. For example, 9-year-old Becky was running down the stairs with a friend, accidentally tripped on her companion's foot, and fell. Because she was extremely self-centered, Becky assumed that the friend had tripped her on purpose, and she started screaming wild accusations at the other girl. Due to her narcissism, Becky was unable to recognize that her fall was an unintentional accident.

After age 10, children who habitually use people for their own benefit may be developmentally arrested at the stage of a subjective, differentiated perspective. To illustrate, Tricia, a senior in high school, was struggling in math, and she sought out a classmate to help her every day during study hall. This informal tutoring continued until Tricia's math grade improved; at that time Tricia discontinued the association without a thought for the feelings of her mentor. This behavior is characteristic of users who may be close to the chosen few who are their friends but who fail to consider the feelings or views of outsiders.

Older children who have delays in social competence may function at the level of the self-reflective, reciprocal perspective. Some of these children may be able to understand the viewpoint of others but are unable to act appropriately on that knowledge. For example, Julio was the center on the basketball team at school. During a playoff game the team decided on the next crucial play, but instead of executing the agreed upon maneuver, Julio did his own thing and "hogged" the ball. He ended up with a disastrous attempt at a slam dunk. On the way back to the showers, Julio was despondent because he had not followed the team's decision and his behavior had led to loss of the game. He knew that his friends were angry and disappointed in him. In this case, Julio was aware of the original team decision and its importance to his teammates but was unable to act upon it; he was able to reflect on the impact his behavior had on his friends' view of him.

Extremely exaggerated cliquishness can be the manifestation of group members locked in the stage of mutual perspective. In these situations, adolescents are able to be intimate and supportive of their group members but tend to reject or ignore other peers. They have a third person perspective when focusing within their group as they negotiate beliefs, values, and rules of how the group functions but are unable to have an objective, third person perspective of how an outsider views the group. As an illustration, four adolescent girls with extreme makeup and attire referred to themselves as the Dreamers. They were inseparable and opinionated, tending to disregard everyone else around them. In their enthusiasm for what occurred in the group, they were clueless about how the rest of the world viewed them and were often oblivious to nasty comments from their peers.

By the teen years a child should be able to take a societal or in-depth perspective on political, moral, and cultural issues. Most teens get into heated discussions of issues as they become increasingly aware of the world around them, and they can talk endlessly about such subjects as the pros and cons of cutting down the Brazilian rainforests, the universal corruption of all politicians, or the justice of a town's curfew for teenagers. Those lacking in social competence often find these conversations frustrating. An example of this point is Ramata and her friends, who were discussing a political topic in the classroom, informally debating the liberal versus the conservative perspective on welfare reform. Ramata had difficulty considering divergent perspectives on the topic and was unable to articulate either viewpoint, making excuses to avoid participating in the discussion. Eventually she opted out entirely by saying, "Why worry about it? It's not our problem. Let Congress decide!"

As children develop and form relationships ranging from casual to intimate, a major achievement is the capacity to take another's perspective — to stand in the other person's shoes. Along with this empathic understanding, children need to be able to display this capacity; in doing so they convey how much they care about others, which in turn fosters mutual reciprocity. The young child may say, "Mommy don't cry," while the older teenager may insist on going with the parents to the vet to put a pet to sleep. Some children with developmental delays in social perspective taking show tendencies to display mild to severe egocentric behavior.

Social and Play Behavior

So far we have discussed the purpose of interactions and social perspective taking as elements of our conceptual framework. The next two chapters address the components of social competence: social and play behavior, self-regulation, communication, prosocial skills, and social decision making.

In this chapter the intrinsic value and therapeutic use of play are discussed, and the different categories of play are detailed. Other factors that influence play behavior are described, including choice of friends, selection of activities, social maturity, degree of playfulness, motivation, parent modeling, and cultural influences. The stages of social play are then delineated, progressing from onlooker play to cooperative play. Finally, the characteristics of play are reviewed from a developmental perspective of early and middle childhood.

In play, the child is actively engaged in a physical or mental activity for the resulting emotional satisfaction. Play is intrinsically motivated and internally controlled, and the child has control over personal actions, particularly in spontaneous play. The child gives attention to the means or process of the play, rather than its end product; thus, play is free of many constraints of objective reality. In some forms of play there exist no externally imposed rules, whereas in other types of play rules exist but can be modified by the participants. The player actively participates in an activity that presents the most appropriate challenge. The best measure of play is the amount of engagement rather than the amount of fun. Indeed, play may involve a spectrum of emotions as well as deep concentration.

Play has intrinsic value in and of itself but also serves a variety of functions. Through play children acquire many developmental skills by exploring their environment, discovering cause and effect relationships, and solving problems. Play advances social competence, particularly through acting out roles using fantasy. Through imaginary play children learn to understand themselves and others while they practice roles that they will later assume. Children also learn to solve emotional problems through play, which allows them to manage anxiety, anger, and inner conflicts in a non-threatening context. An important indicator of a child's emotional well-being is the capacity to be playful.

The expression of emotion during play drives spontaneous engagement and social interaction; positive emotions are generated with particular expressions of joy and playfulness. The practitioner should not confuse play with therapeutic activities that are adult-directed and similar to work, as play has all of the characteristics described previously with the child free of constraints and in control. As a tool of therapy, play is common in clinical and educational settings in which the practitioner designs the environment, structures the activity, and establishes the rules. Each of these alternatives can be legitimately used in clinical work. However, the practitioner must keep these distinctions in mind, choose deliberately when each is indicated, and not confuse the child by calling "work" play.

An example of modified play is the case of 7 year-old Conrad, whose therapeutic goal was to improve coordination and balance. The practitioner placed him in a swing and rocked him back and forth while singing an action-filled song. Conrad responded to this by laughing and smiling. In contrast, 7 year-old Mavis, for whom a practitioner had goals similar to those for Conrad, was given a variety of activities to choose from and chose the swing. Mavis immediately said that she was a pirate on the rocky sea and that the practitioner was trying to capture her ship; she started swinging vigorously while chanting make-believe buccaneer songs. Mavis shouted with delight when she eventually routed the invader with deft maneuvers of the swing. In this scenario, Mavis was involved in true play as creator and director of the fantasy.

Categories of Play

Play can be divided into at least four categories (Parham & Primeau, 1997; Pugmire-Stoy, 1992). These play categories appear in a developmental sequence based initially on sensory and motor experiences, with more cognitive and communicative abilities emerging over time.

Practice play: Activities that afford the pleasurable expression of physical skills.

Constructive play: Activities that build an end product.

Symbolic play: Games made up by individual children usually involving make-believe and imitation.

Games-with-rules: Social games that involve regulations imposed by the group and sanctions for a violation of the rules.

These categories of play reflect a developmental hierarchy, with practice play being the most primitive. Variations of these play behaviors continue and evolve throughout life. Practice play in adulthood may be seen in tennis and in going to the gym, while symbolic play may be expressed through regional theater or dressing up for Halloween parties. Adults participate in many games-with-rules such as playing bridge or being a member of the office bowling league.

Children with special needs often present a very uneven sequence in play development; a child may become arrested at one level and unable to move beyond it, or may even completely miss a specific category. Scattering of skills may occur within a category or among the categories. The following discussion describes the goals that are served in each category and provides examples of issues related to children with delays.

Practice Play

The practice category of play involves actively using motor abilities and the body senses, and is aimed at mastering motor skills and at gaining satisfaction through repetitive, pleasurable activities. The practice play pattern dominates until a child is age 2; afterward it is but one category of play in the child's repertoire. Children with special needs may experience motor-related difficulties that restrict such play; they may move too slowly or too quickly, causing them to avoid physical activities, or they may have trouble holding a pencil, causing them to avoid writing and art activities. Such problems in practice play limit mastery and self-confidence. As a result, these children may not be good at games and sports and are often the last ones chosen to be on a team. A vicious cycle of skill deficit, decreased learning opportunities, and social isolation can lead to repeated failures in the acquisition of practice play.

Constructive Play

This category of play leads to an end product such as is seen in woodworking, block play, and varied art media. Constructive play is possible whenever a child is able to build with materials and begins with simple block building at age 18–20 months. Some children may have difficulty in constructive play if they have limited sensory and motor abilities, cannot create visual images or blue prints of the construction, or are unable to retrieve such stored information.

Jerry, age 5, showed problems with constructive play when he and his friends played with Legos®. While his friends created elaborate structures such as castles and forts, Jerry was struggling with the mechanics of putting the pieces together. He was unable to visualize and construct any structure beyond a primitive vertical tower. As he observed the others' play, Jerry blurted out in frustration, "But it's just a bunch of blocks! I don't see a castle!"

Symbolic Play

This category of play affords opportunities for the child to pretend, imagine, experiment, and recreate meaning in the world. The child can make up and envision roles by acting out parts about himself and others. Feelings can be attributed and role-played, particularly regarding stressful situations. Symbolic play begins during the second year of life and tends to peak at ages 4 and 5, before diminishing during the rest of the life span. This category incorporates dramatic or pretend play as well as fantasy or socio-dramatic play.

Children with communicative problems often experience difficulties in symbolic play. They may remain in a concrete world where objects have restricted and limited purposes. Consequently, their ability to take and give roles and to engage in reciprocal role taking may be deficient. Social limitations related to recognizing and understanding the feelings and perspectives of others may also be present.

Tina is a child with competence in symbolic play. When her baby sister arrived, 8 year-old Tina was consumed with sibling rivalry. At school she worked through her ambivalent feelings about her sister with her peers during recess. During play with her Barbie®, Tina would nurture the doll by combing its hair and dressing it in a favorite outfit; shortly thereafter she would demonstrate her rage by roughly removing the doll's clothes, pulling its hair, and throwing it on the ground. This symbolic play over a period of 2 months contributed considerably to the resolution of Tina's sibling rivalry.

Games-With-Rules

This category enables children to comprehend and use rule-bound behavior. Initially, children develop their own rules and tacitly acknowledge a leader for the group experience. Later, more formal games with established rules emerge, particularly at ages 6 and 7. There are innumerable games-with-rules: board games such as Candy Land®, Lotto®, and Clue®; card games including Old Maid, Solitaire, and War; visually directed fine motor games like jacks, pick-up sticks, and video games; and gross motor activities such as tag, T-ball, hide-and-seek, hopscotch, and jump rope. Children may encounter a myriad of problems that are obstacles to their satisfactory participation in games. Such difficulties include inattention, impulsivity, the inability to understand verbal and abstract commands, and challenges in following directions. As an example, peers did not want to interact with 9-year-old Juan on the playground because he became too wild and disruptive during games of tag. Juan had three major behaviors that interfered with his ability to play cooperatively. First, he had difficulty agreeing with rules that were established by the group; second, he was unable to attend simultaneously to the physical aspects of the task and the ongoing verbal exchange; third, he was a poor loser every time he was tagged out.

Knowing the categories of play contributes to the understanding of a child's developmental status and to planning personalized intervention. Our intervention approach is grounded on an appreciation of the normal activities and leisure pursuits of a child's world. The characteristics of practice play, constructive play, symbolic play and games-with-rules serve as a basis for designing intervention strategies. This information also provides developmental guidelines for evaluating and sequencing treatment over time.

Play-Related Issues

In addition to an appreciation of the categories of play, the practitioner should be aware of a number of other factors that influence the play behavior of children. These factors are wide ranging and include such issues as choice of friends, selection of activities, social maturity, degree of playfulness, motivation and interest, family influences, and cultural factors. Each of these topics is introduced with implications for practice.

Choice of Friends

Children with delays in play skills and social behavior often do not fit in with their peers. They seem younger than their age and often choose playmates who are significantly younger or older, which enables them to play at the level of social maturity they are comfortable with. An egocentric, immature 8-year-old child can dominate younger children. While this older child may be viewed as the big kid on the block, he or she can feel good about taking a younger child under his or her wings and being looked up to by the younger child. At times exceptional children have older playmates who tolerate their immaturity because of their youth. However, some children may seek to avoid play with other children entirely and focus instead on pseudo-adult relationships or overly dependent interactions with adults. At school a teacher may become a social focus, with the child making efforts to engage the teacher at lunch and recess, rather than participating in exchanges with peers. Another scenario includes children who cannot relinquish or share friends and hang on too tightly for fear of losing them.

Selection of Activities

Just as the choice of friends can appear chronologically inappropriate, a child may choose materials, toys, and games that represent younger play levels or are used in perseverative or restricted ways. An absence of play with toys may be seen in aimless wandering and appearing spaced out. Difficulties in self-regulation can interfere with a child's ability to focus on activities and play in an organized manner. At times, a lack of exposure to a rich play environment is the cause of restrictions in activity selection. For example, an impoverished or chaotic home setting can undermine the child's readiness for engagement. Further, delays in motor development may cause restrictions in how children play. For instance, Miles, age 10, was clumsy and preferred to play with preschool telephones and cash registers rather than cooperative group games. Loretta, age 5, was a bright girl with tactile defensiveness. Her tense, hyper-aroused state prevented Loretta from engaging in certain types of activities, and as a result, she tended to withdraw and wander or become controlling.

Social Maturity

Some children are less mature in their language, cognitive, psychosocial, and physical development, and may exhibit irritating behaviors that lead to exclusion, derision, and possible victimization by peers. These children are frequently too self-absorbed and self-focused to help others, or they may lack the confidence and ability to reach out to others in appropriate ways. Self-control is commonly limited, resulting in impulsivity and speaking out of turn. Such children are viewed as unreliable and unpredictable because of their self-centeredness, poor self-control, and impulsivity. As a result, they forget the rules of games from one minute to the next and burst into anger or tears when frustrated by demands. Because difficulties are often present in reading social cues such as facial expressions, these children can laugh or joke at the wrong times or fail to respond to a friend's urgent request to stop an activity (e.g., tickling, roughhousing, teasing). These problems in social adjustment typically lead to the label of childish as a descriptor of behavior.

Motivation and Interest

Although the motivation for social play is usually intrinsic, some children do not seem to exhibit this drive; consequently, they tend to be overly reliant on solitary activities, fantasy, and television. The following are key points to consider regarding children who lack motivation and interest.

- In some circumstances, children are not motivated to become engaged because the social play is too difficult and they lack the necessary skills to take part successfully. Without the requisite developmental skills, these children would rather play alone, pursuing activities such as riding their bikes or reading.

- Some children avoid peer play because of a history of rejection by others. They may gradually lose interest and withdraw, or they may engage in age appropriate activities alone. In both cases, these children are trying to protect themselves from further pain.

- Some children with attentional deficits have difficulty dividing their attention simultaneously between two demands. In social play, these children must consider the ideas of a peer while concurrently maintaining their own. This task is challenging because these children risk forgetting part of their own ideas or lack the skills to integrate the ideas of another into a united plan. Typically, the outcome of the actual play is of lesser quality than originally envisioned; as a result, these children prefer solitary play to an inferior outcome.

- Some children who are intellectually gifted are condescending about playing with same age peers because of their perceived language superiority. Although skilled in the cognitive and language domains, these children may be delayed in their social development, as precocious language development frequently masks real social deficits. Such children often prefer adult interactions to those with peers.

The following are general strategies to promote motivation and interest in sharing play.

- Children must be engaged in play that is both developmentally appropriate as well as chronologically interesting. The best play activities are ones that respect the chronological age of the child: not too "babyish" for older children but modified so that they challenge the abilities of the child at the correct developmental age.

- Competitive elements often need to be lessened, while cooperative exchanges are increased in order to motivate, interest, and teach children. For example, the practitioner can select a game such as cooperative musical chairs, in which all children end up sitting together rather than eliminating children from the game and having one winner.

- Emphasis must also be given to helping children develop constructive leisure time activities and hobbies by discovering their own identities, assets, and strengths.

Degree of Playfulness

Playfulness, characterized by the ability to laugh, fool around, and have fun, is a desirable quality during play activities, and reflects the child's internal motivation, ability to be inventive, and sense of control over the environment. All children show varying degrees of playfulness. Children with special needs may present the extremes of this range, either being too playful and not knowing when to cut it out or being too restricted and unable to "relax and enjoy" the game.

For instance, 8-year-olds Davey and Roxie were engaged in block building. They initially started to collaborate on building one structure but Davey became distracted by his tangential thinking. He automatically fantasized about a wealth of potential constructions, complete with narratives regarding their use. Davey was unable to focus on the specific construction task at hand. Roxie's thinking, on the other hand, was entirely too concrete and restricted to be playful. She overfocused on assembling a tower and ignored all of Davey's suggestions; further, her overall affect was bland, flat, and mechanical. The quality of playfulness for both of these children was distorted, although for different reasons.

In a real sense, playfulness is highly diagnostic of the child's overall functional competence. Evaluation of playfulness becomes a part of the initial assessment of a child's social abilities and can also be used as a marker of change.

Family Influences

The influence of parents, siblings, extended family members, close neighbors, and friends on the socialization of children cannot be overestimated. Children first learn social behaviors in the home within relationships. Parents teach their children social skills both through modeling desired behaviors and direct instruction. Of course, the quality of this modeling and instruction varies among families. In some cases, a child will learn manners, social rules, and moral qualities such as kindness and truthfulness very early; in others, the child's poor social competence seems related to inadequate parental teaching. Sometimes a parent's interpersonal style is not a good match for a given child, meaning that the parent may act in an overbearing, ambiguous, or otherwise inconsistent manner. In other cases, social development is impaired because of the erratic and chaotic nature of the physical environment and family life. At times, the parents may model inappropriate and destructive behaviors that children imitate, such as abusive language, antisocial acts, and generally crude or rude behavior. When assessing a child, the practitioner must remember that the behaviors the child is presenting may reflect, in part, inadequate social skills modeled by the parents. At the same time, the practitioner should avoid the pitfalls of judging parents or blaming them for their child's social conduct.

Cultural and Environmental Influences

Play is intimately influenced by the divergent rules and customs represented by race, ethnicity, class, generational differences, and geographic regions (Hetherington & Parke, 1993). These cultural factors influence variations in social norms, define acceptable and expected social behaviors, and determine styles of teaching and modeling for social conduct. The adequacy of a child's play behavior cannot be fully understood without appreciating the child's cultural background and context. There are many examples of culture's impact on play.

- The degree of eye contact that is considered appropriate varies noticeably among some Native Americans, Asian Americans, and Italian Americans. Depending on the group represented, eye contact may be considered socially attentive or disrespectful.

- A child from a different ethnic, religious, or socio-economic background may find it difficult to participate in imaginative play with age peers with whom he or she does not share common experiences. For example, fantasy themes for symbolic play are typically derived from television and movies. These may be foreign subjects to a child and thus, the child cannot fully participate in resulting play.

  Also, the degree of lively playfulness that is encouraged and accepted at the dinner table varies. In some groups children are expected to sit still and be quiet ("seen but not heard"), while in other groups there is joy having the children animated and playing at and around the dinner table.

- A child who has recently relocated from a different part of the country might need to learn playground rules for the new locale. A game as simple as shooting baskets may have multiple variations and the child has to learn the applicable rules for his or her new environment.

- Some cultures do not place a high value on time spent in play, directing the efforts of children toward household chores and homework instead. In a sense, some of these children may not know how to play or how to be playful due to a lack of experience.

These are only a few samples of the cultural influences that shape play and social encounters. Others that come to mind are a culture's impact on deciding whether or not to greet strangers, determining appropriate tone of voice for various situations, expressing frustration and negotiating conflict, and scheduling play dates. Encounters leading to cultural mismatches can be humorous, embarrassing, or devastating to the child, particularly in adolescence when there is a tremendous need to fit in and avoid embarrassment.

In addition to the social context, the impact of the physical environment must be considered. Physical surroundings dictate the types of play chosen as well as the appropriateness of the play; for instance, running around is acceptable in the park, but not in the visiting room at the hospital. At times the broad physical context has a major influence on play. To illustrate, some children living in urban poverty may have restricted access to play experiences as parents may be fearful when their children are outside and keep them indoors in rather crowded conditions. In contrast, a child in a remote rural area may have ample room and safety for active physical exploration but may have very few playmates.

The example of Rocky is instructive, as he had an enviable environment that had the best of all worlds from his perspective. Rocky grew up living on a cul-de-sac with plenty of kids his age and near a small field that had a set of monkey bars. Beyond the field were woods with worn paths. This physical setting invited Rocky to play alone as well as with others in endless adventures. Each site invited a different type of practice play, symbolic play, and game-with-rules. This environment was free of danger and, consequently, had little need for adult oversight and supervision. Such experiences shaped Rocky's play repertoire, his views regarding the value of play, and his personal sense of competence and self-reliance. A long-term impact was seen in his role as a parent many years later, when he modeled his love and enjoyment of play with his children and nurtured a family atmosphere that recreated the feelings of his boyhood.

Stages of Social Play

Parten (1932), one of the early observers of the social play of children, described a developmental sequence in the stages of play that has relevance to current practice. This sequence progresses from a status of solitary play to some interaction with others and ends with cooperative play that has a sense of group belonging. Each new stage of play is added to the ones that came before; previous stages are not discarded, but retained to enrich the child's repertoire. For example, onlooker play seen in toddlers is retained in adulthood as the viewing of spectator sports such as boxing and football. The developmental sequence is as follows:

Unoccupied Play Behavior — The child momentarily watches activity in the environment but is basically unaware of others. When not attending, the child engages in body play, gross motor activity, or gazing about the room. This type of play is characteristic of an infant.

Onlooker play — The child watches the play of others but does not participate actively. Attention is on the play objects held by the other children as well as the kids themselves. This play is initially seen at ages 1 to 2 years. Observations of a concert, athletic event, the circus, or the movies are examples of onlooker play of adults.

Solitary independent play — This is a brief phase generally seen in children around age 2. The child plays alone with objects, and there is no interaction with others or change of play in response to other children. This is a transitional stage between onlooker and parallel play during which the child is heavily focused on playing with objects.

Parallel play — In this stage, the child plays beside peers, often with similar toys. Although others influence activity, there is no direct interaction between the child and other children, although there seems to be a feeling of "playing together" due to the physical closeness and similarity of activity. Parallel play is best seen between ages 2 to 3. An example in adulthood is a couple who tend their separate garden patches; he grows the vegetables while she grows the flowers. Another example is this couple relaxing in the evening as he reads and she does a crossword puzzle.

Associative play — During this stage children play with each other, but there is no organization of the activity; they interact together, but the play is not dependent on any one child's participation. Although there is a broad understanding of the play theme, each child primarily follows his own ideas and wishes, never working out common ground rules. There is little influence of one child on the behavior of another. The children may exchange toys or imitate each other, but typically the children act individually, with the focus on their association and not the activity per se. Associative play commonly appears around age 3½ and is prominent in the play of the child at age 4.

A good example of this stage is children playing at the sandbox or housekeeping corner with little sharing. They enjoy being together but are not necessarily socially engaged. For instance, Billy and Joelle, almost 4 years of age, were playing with trains. Billy was building a bridge for the train to go under, while Joelle was extending the train tracks around the room. They chose and pursued their tasks individually, without consulting one another. Periodically, they traded train cars as they wandered around each other's construction.

Cooperative play — During this stage, children play in an organized manner to achieve a purpose such as carrying out formal games or making an item. The children assume organizational roles in order to accomplish the task, and there is shared pursuit of a goal and division of labor. In games, the rules are mutually accepted, although they are open for revision among the players. Frequently, one or two leaders direct activity. In addition, there is a sense of belonging to the group. Cooperative play is evident at age 5 and becomes increasingly sophisticated and elaborated with time. Examples of cooperative play during middle childhood include games such as bingo, Monopoly®, tag, kickball, softball, and four-square, along with activities such as making a haunted house for Halloween and forming a club. Similarly, adults demonstrate cooperative play in board games, team sports, and shared leisure activities.

The stated age expectations are general guidelines for the developmental sequence of social play. In reality, achievement of these milestones varies from child to child. Likewise, these stages are overlapping; as the child matures at one skill level, the next stage emerges. Many children with delays and disabilities get stuck at the level of associative play, and although they may play in the midst of a cooperative group, they are unable to play in a purposeful and organized manner, accept rules, assume organizational roles, interact collaboratively, or develop a sense of group belonging. They seem to have difficulty keeping up with the give-and-take interaction of cooperative play. The practitioner must remember the stages of social play during assessment and intervention planning. When the level of social play is overlooked in the assessment process, the practitioner may overestimate the social development of the child and assume the child has skills in play that are absent or that are only emerging.

Play in Early and Middle Childhood

In addition to knowing the stages of social play, the practitioner must understand the characteristics of play behavior at different ages of development in order to choose appropriate activities and modify them for intervention purposes. The following tables detail typical behaviors to expect at each age and can be useful in the construction of a play experience for specific children. Adapted from the work of Linda Florey and Sandra Greene (1997), Table 4.1 lists the characteristics of play in preschool children centered around issues of peer relationships and play interests, while Table 4.2 describes the peer relationships, rules and games, and play interests of children in the middle childhood years.

Table 4.1
Characteristics of Play During Early Childhood

Ages 3–5

Peer Relationships	• Interactions increasingly frequent, sustained, and social
	• Enjoyment of being with peers as play becomes more group oriented
	• Preference of certain children and initial formation of cliques
	• Differentiation of roles in dramatic play, that is, one person the mother, another the baby, etc.
	• Participation in longer and more complex dramatic sequences
	• Use of speech during dramatic play to ascribe action and identify objects to self and others
	• Involvement in games in which all players take turns
	• Development of bragging and name calling
Play Interests	• Common interests include block and construction play and pretend play
	• Imaginative play requires more complete and realistic costumes
	• Real world becomes more fascinating with an increased incidence of "why" questions
	• Interest in results of efforts or products but are not very process oriented
	• Development of pride in achievements; may want products untouched with one's name on them

Reprinted and adapted from written material, Annual Conference, American Occupational Therapy Association, Chicago. © Linda Lory, 1996.

Table 4.2
Characteristics of Play During Middle Childhood

Peer Relationships

Children 6–8	• Group very important — adjusting to group controls • Informal "gang" with few formal rules and rapid turnover in membership • Learning to work with others although little skill in cooperation • Leadership of group changes rapidly • Helpful to age mates but fighting is frequent • Common to have teasing and ganging up • Separation of the sexes
Children 9–12	• Varied groups important — join many and establish cliques • More formal, highly structured groups with special membership and elaborate rituals for meetings • Clubs with passwords and secret rules • Organized activities such as scouts and teams • Conformity to peer codes • Competition with others • Best friends — becoming more stable

Rules and Games

Children 6–8	• Need to win is placed above rules of the game • Prefer to make up own rules and play until they win • Vague about how rules operate • Enjoy voting but have trouble accepting majority rule • Fail to understand that rules apply equally to everyone • Cheating and tattling are common
Children 9–12	• Children want to make and break rules. • Children want to decide how rules and turns will be determined. • There are frequent arguments over what is fair play and what is cheating. • Children are more conscientious of rules and obeying them. • Rules becoming more relative and flexible. • Children have a greater capacity to accept majority decisions.

Play Interests

Children 6–8	• Dramatic play gradually decreases, but there is still an interest in costumes. • Quantity is important in collecting, and nature items are popular. • Crafts require encouragement and sequencing of steps to complete the activity. • There is an increased emphasis on practice to develop mastery of skills. • Children exhibit a tendency to be critical of their own work as well as that of others.
Children 9–12	• Interest in dramatic play in groups increases. • Collecting and trading lead to big collections. • Children explore many crafts and hobbies with expanding satisfaction. • Children enjoy board games and physical activities.

Reprinted and adapted from written material, Annual Conference, American Occupational Therapy Association, Chicago. © Linda Florey, 1996.

Additional Components of Social Competence

Self-Regulation

Chapter 4 addressed play and social behavior as an important component of social competence in the conceptual framework. This chapter focuses on the other four critical components of self-regulation, communication, prosocial skills, and social decision making.

In self-regulation, a child has an internal drive to achieve a balance or homeostasis. From the earliest months of life, an infant demonstrates a tendency to regulate the tension generated when interacting socially with others, modulating its engagement through such adaptive patterns as gaze aversion, sucking on its hand, yawning, adjusting breathing, vocalizing, and thrashing its limbs. Demands increase markedly over time for children to become involved with more diverse activities and a greater number of people. Such demands require a more complex regulation of the self with the external world. As noted in Table 5.1, this self-regulation influences at least five important dimensions: arousal, attention, physical control, flexibility, and affect. These are areas of vulnerability for many children with social difficulties.

Table 5.1
Dimensions of Self-Regulation

Arousal	Attention	Physical Control
High	Selective Attention	Postures and Mannerisms
Low	Shift of Attention	Physical Proximity
Fluctuating	Divided Attention	Vocal Tone
	Allocation of Attention	Impulse Control
	Eye Contact	Activity Level

Flexibility	Affect	
Adaptable Thinking	Degree and Intensity	
Transitioning	Gratification Delay	
Timing and Pacing		

Arousal

A fundamental human capacity is a person's ability to self-modulate the level of arousal or alertness. Even in the newborn, there are smooth shifts between states of sleep and wakefulness. A fluid and dynamic interplay between the two parts of the autonomic nervous system, the sympathetic and parasympathetic, exists in normal functioning. The sympathetic nervous system activates and energizes the child, and is reflected by such measurable indicators as increased heart rate, respiration, and blood pressure; in its full state, the sympathetic system causes a fight or flight response. In contrast, the parasympathetic system relaxes and calms the body and has the opposite signs of decreased heart rate, respiration, and blood pressure; in its full state, there is a tendency to shut down and withdraw. In interaction with the environment, the balance between these two systems helps to regulate the child's level of arousal.

To maintain social engagement, an optimal degree of arousal is necessary. This level of alertness is seen in the 3-year-old child who is playful, exploring, interacting, taking appropriate risks, and freely separating from caregivers without trauma. The child is able to manage successfully the multisensory preschool environment. This capacity for modulation of arousal is elaborated over the years as the child learns to shift between structure and non-structure, quiet and active times, and solitary and social settings.

There is a normal continuum of arousal along which the child should be able to function. For instance, a child must be on high arousal in the presence of an attacking dog and on low arousal just before naptime. When the level of arousal is continuously mismatched with environmental demands, there are grounds for concern, whether the mismatch is high, low, or fluctuating levels of arousal. For example, a child who is overaroused is not able to monitor his energy at the same level as his playmates; he may become chaotic, run around, and fail to follow the rules of the game.

Attention

Attention is a brain function involving the ability to concentrate thoughts and sensations on what is essential for as long as is necessary. The capacity to focus attention on what is important while ignoring irrelevant background stimuli is called selective attention. Another aspect is the ability to shift attention between stimuli; for instance, to be able to switch focus among speakers during a lively conversation. Another important function is the ability to divide attention between two simultaneous stimuli such as listening to the teacher and taking notes. Allocation of attention is the time spent in maintaining a focus as well as the amount of energy required to sustain it. It reflects the degree of effort it takes to maintain the required attention span and influences vigilance or the readiness to respond. For example, a child must be able to wait with anticipation for the next set of instructions in a test.

Individuals with social deficits may have problems with any of these aspects of attention. Children who have problems attending are not sensitive to details and often have difficulty reading the social situation and profiting from feedback. Indeed, many of these children are unaware when they make a social mistake. Their communication pattern tends to be rather staccato, with frequent starts and stops in the conversation (Levine, 1987). Problems in attention are often associated with distractibility.

Appropriate eye contact is expected during social exchanges. Eye contact is not to be confused with staring. Typically, a speaker makes visual regard at the beginning of a sentence or point, deviates his or her gaze while talking, and then re-establishes visual regard when completing the sentence or point. As always, cultural differences must be considered. Some cultures discourage children from making eye contact with an authority figure because such behavior is considered disrespectful, while other cultures encourage children to look at others eye to eye. Patterns of abnormal eye contact include staring at points away from the speaker, complete lack of visual regard, and excessive eye activity such as blinking, squinting, and wandering eye movements. For some children, eye contact is limited because they are not able to process visual input simultaneously with auditory input; basically, some children cannot look and listen at the same time.

Physical Control

Modulation of posture and movement is another important aspect of self-regulation. Children with interpersonal difficulties may demonstrate atypical body postures and mannerisms that convey a non-verbal message that undercuts their social acceptability. Common patterns include slumping, rigid tensing of the trunk, wiggling, finger chewing, clothes picking, nail biting, hair twirling, and nervous tics. Various factors contribute to the presence of these behaviors, including anxiety, sensory defensiveness, and social stress. In addition, some children may have difficulty in maintaining an appropriate physical proximity to others; they may tend to position themselves too close or too far away from others by the standards of conventional social distance. For instance, Jacob almost insists on being in the teacher's lap when interacting rather than sitting close by.

Another example of self-regulation in physical control is a person's appropriate use of his or her voice. Vocal quality is made up of two aspects, the volume of speech and the emotional tenor. Some children speak too quietly or too loudly, or may fluctuate between these two extremes. For others, the issue is primarily that their voice has an unattractive or annoying emotional tone, such as whiny, challenging, condescending, or angry.

Physical impulsiveness is a breakdown in self-regulation, in which children behave without thinking, planning, or anticipating the consequences. For example, in a game children may know the rules and be able to explain them but appear incapable of control, acting too quickly and without sufficient previewing. If these children think of something, they do it. Examples of impulsivity include interrupting, blurting out, talking excessively, and failing to wait for one's turn. Such impulsiveness undermines the child's ability to predict social consequences, produce effective adaptive interactions, and control aggression. Hyperactivity is often seen in children with impulsivity and related problems in physical control. The combination of hyperactivity and impulsivity can cause an abruptness and bluntness in the child's interactive style; this undermines the indirect, friendship-building give-and-take that is so important in developing relationships.

Flexibility

Another problem in self-regulation is inflexibility in behavior. School-age children may have problems in letting go of the immediate focus, as well as problems in committing to new situations. Children who have delays in social perspective taking, and who find it difficult to free themselves from their egocentricity in particular, tend to display this behavior. Their narcissism blocks attempts toward flexible thinking and can lead to problems in social reciprocity and communication. Inflexible children often have trouble in transitions and shifting between activities; they are insistent on following familiar routines and activities and resist moving on to new ones. Because they cannot entertain the ideas and suggestions of other people, these children are not risk takers and are not considered fun.

Affect

The ability to share internal emotional experience is essential to social communication. A child needs to have a wide variety of emotions and moods that can be modulated in their expression. Many children with social delays demonstrate extremes of emotion, at an explosive pace, and with greater intensity than is developmentally appropriate (Goldstein & Goldstein, 1995). They seem to be on an emotional roller coaster. Some of these children cry at the least provocation, and their anger seems to have no limits. Minor disappointments can evoke profound sadness; likewise, a sense of joy can border on near hysteria. For instance, when Samona accomplishes a task with success, she immediately responds with laughter that quickly escalates into ear-piercing shrieks. Such behavior is very alienating to peers who find it not only inappropriate but also unsettling because of its unpredictability. Although varying temperamentally from intense to laid back, all children must learn to regulate a range of emotional states and expressions needed in the fast-moving, complex world of peer interaction.

Some children with problems in the social arena have difficulty delaying rewards and working towards a long-term goal, leaving tasks unfinished because they require immediate gratification. These children are very hard to satisfy and require consistent and frequent payoffs. There is an intensely creative quality to some of these children that is appealing, however peers frequently find their behavior frustrating over time because of the lack of closure. For instance, 7-year-old Chucky was working on a collaborative scout badge project with his friends, and he came up with an idea that everyone endorsed enthusiastically. Because the project lasted a number of weeks longer than planned, Chucky became very impatient and wanted to abandon it in favor of a new project. This behavior was typical of Chucky who was big on ideas and short on follow through.

Communication

Communication is another component of social competence depicted in the conceptual framework. Communication is the process of understanding and sharing meaning, and serves at least four separate functions:

1. Physical safety is enhanced when communication serves to protect personal space and possessions. The child also elicits adult caregiving by expressing fears or complaints of aches and pains.

2. Communication increases personal awareness. Children gather information about who they are through the ways others treat them. For example, a child decides that she is bright and funny because her friends routinely laugh at her witty stories. This ability is dependent upon intact verbal and non-verbal language skills.

3. Through communication we also purposefully present ourselves to others. Our behavior is influenced by the impressions others have of us, as well as how we would like to be perceived. This issue becomes very important as children enter the teenage years.

4. We communicate to achieve personal ambitions, attempting to persuade others to agree with us or to act on our behalf. For example, a child may actively convince a peer to join him in a game he wishes to play. Persuasion can also be used to entice a child to join one clique and reject another.

Given these broad functions of communication, children with language deficits often experience significant breakdowns in their social performance. Of the five components of social competence in the conceptual framework, problems in communication evoke the greatest anxiety in these children. Challenges in communication and language are common but often go unrecognized. The presenting behaviors are typically accepted as the primary problem instead of the language deficit; the child is seen as being shy, stubborn, slow, or uncooperative. As social communication becomes more sophisticated with age, language difficulties become more intrusive over time.

The following is a list of some of the most frequently seen communication-related problems in children with social limitations.

- **Problems in Discourse.** Children with social challenges often have narrative disorganization, experiencing difficulty in producing descriptive prose orally or in writing. Typically, there are problems in starting, ordering, and concluding thoughts. For example, a child may have difficulty initiating and maintaining a topic, extending a topic, switching a topic, and repairing a breakdown in conversation. Communication is often tangential, rambling, excessively detailed, or lacking in substance. Children may appear quiet and shy due to an expressive language disorder preventing initiation of conversation. Children who have good pretend play skills appear to develop more complex communication and use of language, and are more responsive to the cues of others.

- **Problems in Pragmatics.** Pragmatics involves the appropriate use of language to accomplish various ends in differing social contexts. Children need to know how to express their intentions for varied situations. Pragmatic skills acquired in childhood enable children to operate in wider social circles and in a greater variety of discourse genres. Children must adapt messages according to audience, audience's knowledge of the subject, and audience needs. Children with pragmatic deficits have trouble discerning a speaker's true meaning or intentions. Knowing when to speak, knowing when to listen, and maintaining appropriate eye contact are key components of pragmatics; lack of these components leads to a breakdown in interpretation of the social context (often an overly literal interpretation) (Levine, 1987). Children with pragmatic difficulties often lack the ability to take the perspective of the listener and also have trouble effectively expressing their needs to others. Tending to speak in declarative statements, these children do not functionally use language to request actions and objects, to comment, to describe, to clarify, to share information, to request information, to disagree, and to express beliefs. The lack of this elaborative use of language may be related to failure to understand language in its social context. These children do not consider how social context can alter the meaning of sentences, or discern variations that reflect a speaker's age, perspective, or point of view.

- **Breakdown in Speaker-Listener Responsibility.** Communication is a two-way process that requires not only an able speaker but an able listener as well. Learning to listen is as important as learning to speak. There is a social responsibility for listening that involves truly attending to the other and fluidly shifting from expressive to receptive language. Communication is by definition reciprocal, requiring turn taking and the provision of clear messages. The speaker must also recognize the non-verbal messages the listener sends when there is a breakdown in the conversation.

Some children with social difficulties are so egocentric that they automatically assume that the listener has adequate background information on the topic at hand and fail to provide critical information related to their discussion. In addition to egocentricity, a breakdown in speaker-listener responsibility may result from poor auditory memory or attention. Behaviorally, these children blurt out what is on their mind due to the inability to mentally hold thoughts while listening rather than true impulsivity. There is a sense of urgency to express the thoughts before they are lost. Finally, the speaker has the obligation to provide non-verbal cues that are clear and compatible with the verbal message. At the same time, the listener is obliged to notice and interpret the non-verbal information such as facial expression, gestures, body language, or degree of eye contact.

- **Problems in Word Finding.** A common social difficulty is the child's inability to retrieve words during conversations, constituting a lack of systematic and effective retrieval strategies for self-expression. These children may have a deficient vocabulary or an enriched one. For one child language will be sparse and lack elaboration, while another may not be identified because he or she offers understandable ideas without any apparent difficulty, although from the child's perspective the word selection was not optimal and the child is left feeling frustrated. Word finding problems are usually associated with slow and delayed responses. Because efficiency and speed of communication are critical to social success, poor timing is a major deficit.

In summary, children respond differently if they are aware of their language problems. Children who are conscious of the difficulty will tend to be fearful and hyper-vigilant, appearing wide-eyed and wary as they struggle to comprehend the drift of the chatter around them. These children show considerable anxiety about the accuracy of what they hear and how they should respond, and there is a persistent worry about looking foolish, resulting in being ashamed. Children who are not particularly aware of their language problem exhibit a tendency to look "out of it" and disconnected. These children catch on to the pattern of turn taking in conversation but are unable to participate in the reciprocal give and take with others. They wait for a lull in the conversation to make a comment, then sit back and wait for another lull to jump in with a new thought. These offerings may have varying relevance to the ongoing topic.

Prosocial Skills

Prosocial skills are the positive behaviors that facilitate relating such as helping, sharing, and turn taking. These social attributes are the learned "civilizing" abilities that make children welcomed members of a community, and include rules of social engagement and politeness such as giving compliments, directing the conversation to others, and offering an invitation to play. Prosocial skills also include self-marketing (promoting yourself as socially desirable), accurately reading the tone of a conversation, knowing how to effectively get your way, being conversant in the current topics and lingo of the peer group, and developing an altruistic caring and respect for others. The individual welcomes the contribution of others, interacts with empathy, and minimizes the hurt feelings of peers.

Standard social skills curricula that are found in schools emphasize teaching prosocial behaviors. These commercially available programs provide a list of positive social behaviors to be taught through direct instruction, modeling, and practice. An example is the list from the *Social Skills Rating System* of Gresham and Elliott (1990); Table 5.2 presents the social skills that they address under the rubric of Cooperation, Assertion, and Self-Control. From our perspective, some of these skills, such as "finishes assignments," "keeps desk clean," and "produces correct work" are really desired classroom behaviors and not prosocial abilities per se. However, most of the items in the Assertion and Self-Control sections can be considered prosocial in nature and used outside of classroom situations.

Table 5.2
Social Skills of Gresham and Elliott

Cooperation	Finishes assignments
	Uses time appropriately
	Attends to instruction
	Easily makes transitions
	Produces correct work
	Ignores peer distractions
	Follows directions
	Puts work away
	Uses free time acceptably
	Keeps desk clean
Assertion	Initiates conversations
	Introduces self
	Questions unfair rules
	Invites others to join
	Tells when treated unfairly
	Makes friends
	Gives compliments to peers
	Says nice things about self
	Volunteers to help peers
	Joins ongoing activity
Self-Control	Controls temper with peers
	Compromises in conflict
	Responds appropriately when hit
	Controls temper with adults
	Receives criticism well
	Responds to teasing
	Accepts peers' ideas
	Responds to peer pressure
	Gets along with people
	Gets along with peers

Source: *Social Skills Rating System (SSKS): Teacher Form, Elementary Level* by Frank Gresham and Stephen Elliot © 1990 American Guidance Service, Inc., 4201 Woodland Road, Circle Press, MN 55014-1796. www.agsnet.com

Table 5.3 is a roster of prosocial skills that we have generated. Based on a compilation of the most frequently targeted behaviors taught in published social skills programs, the list is divided into Social Conversation (skills that depend on the heavy use of language) and Interpersonal Behaviors (skills that depend more upon directed action). Although this distinction is somewhat artificial, it helps to divide the list into more manageable sections. The table is also divided into three columns. If you review by column each section (Social Conversation and Interpersonal Behaviors) of the table you can ascertain a continuum of skills from simple to complex; for instance, saying "thank you" precedes giving and accepting compliments, which is followed by giving and accepting criticism. In another example, joining another in play precedes joining a new group, which is followed by joining a variety of groups. This table can be used in the assessment process to target behaviors that require intervention and can also serve as a guide for designing activities that will elicit these desired skills.

Table 5.3
Roster of Prosocial Skills

Social Conversation

Greeting	Sharing minimum information	Sharing personal details,
Introducing self	Introducing others	feelings, values
Asking other's name	Asking details about another	Expressing self spontaneously
Asking permission	Commenting on other's ideas	Respecting other's contributions
Saying thank you	Giving and accepting help	Directing conversation to others
Asking for help	Taking turns talking	Giving and accepting criticism
Answering questions		Giving and accepting apologies

Interpersonal Behaviors

Joining another in play	Generating and implementing	Eliciting experiences and
Following rules established	rules with others	ideas of others
by others	Sharing experiences	Managing various forms
Sharing objects, taking	and ideas	of ostracism
turns in a game	Managing exclusion from	Responding with empathy
Managing teasing	a group	Rewarding self through
Recognizing feelings	Understanding feelings	positive self-statements
Recognizing strengths	Rewarding self through	Dealing with winning, losing,
Joining a new group	concrete means	and peer pressure
	Joining a variety of groups	
	Monitoring other group members	
	in adherence with rules	

The following scenario demonstrates the importance of prosocial skills to support peer play. Diane, who was playing a heated game of RISK™ with a group of children divided into teams of three, quickly determined what she thought was the best move for her team. She was certain it would result in large territories for the team and put them way ahead of the competition. Her playmates were unable to grasp the complexity and advantages of her plan, and they pressed for an alternative move. But Diane insisted that her plan be adopted; she refused to yield to the majority, and she brought the entire game to a halt.

Diane forgot that the purpose of the game was to have fun. She became fixated on winning and cared only about having the perfect move. Diane ignored the critical prosocial skills of getting along with peers, accepting the ideas of others, and responding appropriately to peer pressure. Her lack of prosocial skills led Diane to undermine the game and over time ostracize herself from the group.

Social Decision Making

Social decision making is inherent in everyday living and reflects ways of thinking about, ordering, and managing the social world. Social decision making is the child's process of making choices that govern behavior in relation to others. Children are faced by countless challenges in the social arena: how to ask a friend over after school; how to deal with a bully; how to handle situations on the school bus; how to decide who goes first in a game; how to complete a collaborative science fair project; how to avoid a fight. Decision making is a high-level cognitive task, very much grounded on the other components of social competence (social and play behavior, prosocial skills, self-regulation, and communication), and is readily compromised when there are difficulties in the other domains.

There are five basic steps of social decision making. These steps, or variations of them, are widely reported in the literature as ways to solve interpersonal problems (Elias & Clabby, 1989; Goldstein, 1995).

1. **Identify the problem.** The child defines the problem in terms of what happened, with whom, and when.

2. **Generate alternatives.** The child brainstorms as many solutions as possible to address the problem, with the emphasis on production of alternatives and not their feasibility.

3. **Consider the consequences.** The child examines the positive and negative outcomes of each alternative solution, and, if possible, the short and long-term consequences.

4. **Choose and implement the best alternative.** Based on the consideration of consequences, the child chooses the best solution and implements it. This requires identifying who, what, when, where, and how the solution will occur. Note that the definition of best solution varies from individual to individual.

5. **Evaluate the results.** Determine the outcome of the implemented alternative. Did it achieve the desired results? Upon reflection, was it the best solution? Could this alternative be used again in the future? Is further action warranted?

Here is an example of these steps in action. Three children were trying to determine what to do. The children identified a current problem as "What should we play first?" Next, each child generated alternative preferences: play with Barbies; ride bikes; watch a videotape. Then, the three discussed the consequences of their alternatives, such as "Riding bikes takes too much time." They decided that the best alternative was to play with Barbies because "It is the most fun when we are together!" and "We can watch videos anytime alone!" At the end of the visit, all three children were bubbling over with excitement about playing together again: "It was such fun!"

Curricula are available to teach social decision making to children. The cognitive problem-solving approach usually emphasizes direct teaching, modeling, practice, and coaching. This training is most suited to motivated children with solid cognitive and language skills. It must be adapted to small steps of learning with young children and those with significant delays. This cognitive approach has the advantage of teaching children a general strategy for managing the unlimited variety of challenging social situations but does not address the possibility that the child has problems with play development, self-regulation, and communication. Consequently, our approach categorizes social decision making as one component among five that contributes to social competence.

In our approach, the decision-making questions are asked in the context of the ongoing involvement in play activities. There is a pause for reflection at each of the major steps in the activity, and in this manner the decision-making process is grounded in a concrete activity as it unfolds. The role of the practitioner is to serve as a coach for this thinking process.

An afternoon playgroup comprised of five boys who usually played alone can serve as an illustration. Each of the boys gravitated to their favorite toy trucks in an open area of the room and immediately began to crash the trucks into each other. One of the boys, Mark, repeatedly tried to persuade the others to build a highway for the trucks out of blocks but received no response. The practitioner stepped in, paused the play, and commented that the children's interactions appeared stuck and that no one was listening to Mark. The practitioner asked the group what other ideas they could think of for playing with the trucks. When crashing remained the preferred theme, they were asked why this type of play was a good idea and why it might be a bad idea. Some of the boys commented that by crashing the trucks together, the trucks could get broken; plus, crashing was noisy, and the play bothered other children in the room. This discussion led the group members to change the play to Mark's suggestion.

In this example the practitioner coached the children beyond a repetitive level of play to a more sophisticated level of interaction. By discussing the merits and consequences of their play, the practitioner helped enable the children to determine and implement an alternative solution, as well as progress the level of play and communication between the boys in the playgroup.

Characteristics of Children With Social Difficulties

Major Problems in Social Competence

So far we have discussed the nature of social competence, the early factors that contribute to mature social behavior, and introduced the conceptual framework that is the basis for assessment and intervention, providing a comprehensive perspective on a child's social effectiveness in the context of the home, school, and community. This chapter addresses the primary social problems addressed by the conceptual framework in greater depth. For each of the five components we have provided a list of topical areas that are needed for social functioning and a complimentary list describing some of the underlying difficulties. This format organizes observations and presents problems in useful categories; it also facilitates easy reference for program planning and enables the practitioner to put the conceptual framework to work.

Delays in Social and Play Behavior

The following list presents the common problems found in the areas of social and play behavior.

Types of Play The child is delayed in a stage of play, such as interacting at a parallel or associative level of play at an age when a cooperative level of play may be expected.

Choice of Friends The child does not have age appropriate friendships; friends are markedly younger or older than the child, or the child prefers interactions with adults.

Selection of Activities The child's choice of activities does not match the interests of his or her peers, such as enjoying toys meant for younger children. There is a limited repertoire of play activities; it is expressed through behavior such as resisting group games and insisting on construction tasks. The child routinely chooses the same role, such as being the leader or boss.

Social Maturity The child exhibits the behavior of a younger child, such as whining and tantrums, and demonstrates exaggerated egocentricity, such as demanding attention and insisting on playing the game "my way." Age appropriate social behaviors are lacking with peers and adults, evidenced by behaviors such as verbal intrusions into the conversation of others and the absence of social graces and manners. The child appears asocial and uninterested in interpersonal relationships, exhibiting behavior such as playing alone in the midst of peers.

Degree of Playfulness Playfulness is characteristic of all ages and readily lost with stress or excessive challenges to the child. Traits of playfulness include joy, creativity, imagination, and flexibility, along with the energy level to support them. Impairment in playfulness can be seen in one or more of the following traits: flat or sad affect; lethargy; lack of captivation in the excitement of others; failure to see the humor and fun in situations; and absence of novelty in play.

Motivation and Interest The child may demonstrate low or inconsistent motivation and interest; there may also be a lack of persistence (e.g., not seeing tasks through to their end). Alternately, the child's motivation can be too excessive, resulting in difficulty terminating an activity.

Difficulties in Self-Regulation

The following list presents the common problems found in the area of self-regulation.

Arousal and Attention The child's arousal level is often depressed, elevated, unstable, or unpredictable. The child may be inattentive or possess a brief and inconsistent attention span, causing the child to miss an array of social information. The child may also tend to focus on unimportant sights and sounds.

Non-Verbal Communication The child is unaware of the non-verbal messages sent through his or her own body posture, gesture, and facial expression, and has a tendency to miss the nonverbal communication of others. The child misjudges personal space, tending to be too physically intrusive or distant (stands too close or too far away when speaking, and initiates uninvited physical contact such as touching or bumping into others).

Activity Level The child's activity level is too high or too low for given situations; for example, the child's activity level is too low for a fast-paced sport. Disorganized behavior is marked in some children.

Regulation of Emotions The child may have a constricted or exaggerated range of emotional expression. Lability may be present. The child may have an ongoing problem with the modulation of affective tone. Also, the child may have difficulty recovering from emotional upset, including an inability to self-comfort.

Monitoring Tone of Voice The child's tone of voice may be too loud, too soft, or fluctuating, and the child may be unaware of his or her voice's volume. The voice quality may be unusual, such as breathy, shrill, or grating.

Flexibility Inflexibility is a major problem for many children. The inflexible child is frequently rigid, repetitious, and controlling, and has problems with transitions and shifting between activities. These characteristics interfere with the negotiation and reciprocity that occurs naturally in play and social exchange. The child may be boring as a play partner due to insistence on repeating familiar routines.

Deficits in Communication

The following list presents the common problems found in the area of communication.

Discourse Skills The child has difficulty in initiating, maintaining, and extending a topic. The child also has problems in switching topics and repairing a breakdown in conversation.

Pragmatic Skills The child has a deficit in the functional use of language. A problem exists in one or more of the following skills needed to achieve social ends: requesting; commenting; sharing; describing; clarifying; and disagreeing.

Provide Clear Messages The child delivers unclear messages, with poor progression from beginning to end. He or she often makes an erroneous assumption of shared information, resulting in the child omitting important details. Another pattern is that the child shares an excessive amount of information to the point that the listener is unable to determine what information is pertinent.

Taking Turns Talking There are a number of common problems in this area. These include: limitations in building on and extending the topic of the other person; a tendency to dominate a conversation and not listen to the other person; a breakdown in turn taking when there is more than one speaking partner; poor comprehension of the conversation of others; a limited repertoire of topics for discussion; a passive or shy personality that prevents the child from entering conversations; and a resistance to taking turns for fear of losing his or her thought.

Storytelling Storytelling is a common occurrence in childhood and promotes learning how to make small talk. In this context, storytelling is about personal events in the narrator's life. Sample deficits include a lack of emotional interest, a story line that drifts and becomes tangential, and the speaker's resistance to any interruption.

Persuasion A child may have difficulties in being persuasive for a number of reasons. The child may be bossy and try to steamroll his or her ideas onto others, or may be too timid and fail to try to persuade others at all. The child may not be able to read the cues of the listener, or may lack flexibility of thinking so that he or she fails to generate different strategies for presenting the plan. The child may allow insufficient time for a response because he or she is in too much of a hurry, or may show a deficit in any of the fundamental components of communication, such as pragmatic and discourse skills.

Decreased Competence in Prosocial Skills

The following list presents the common problems found in the area of prosocial skills.

Greeting and Complimenting Others The child tends to omit greetings and intrude into ongoing interactions. Greetings given may be inappropriate. The child typically does not offer compliments or may discount commendable efforts.

Giving and Receiving Feedback *Giving:* The child provides negative feedback in an abrasive, abrupt, or sometimes purposefully hurtful way, or the child may be ambiguous and timid in offering such feedback.

Receiving: The child may not register or understand negative feedback; for example, he or she may not pick up on cues to stop talking. In contrast, the child may react defensively to feedback or choose to ignore it.

Asking for and Providing Information The child may not recognize the need for additional information and therefore may not ask for it. In addition, the child may ask the wrong person or ask in an offensive style. The child may provide information to others in an arrogant manner, be disorganized, or present an unconvincing statement that is consequently ignored.

Extending an Offer of Inclusion The child may not invite others to join in an activity or may do so in a demanding way. The child may rudely include one person and not another. Of equal importance is being able to exclude a child in a graceful manner, such as telling the child that he or she can join the game at the break. Problems occur when the child is too abrupt (such as saying, "Not now!"), or too demeaning in how another is excluded (such as telling the excluded child, "You're too clumsy").

Negotiating Conflict Situations The child may avoid conflict at all costs or may dominate and aggravate the situation. The child may show a lack of flexible reciprocity or give-and-take in an exchange. Often children are impatient and egotistical in their negotiation and ask for adult intervention in a tattle-tale fashion.

Following Rules Made by Others The child tries to modify rules to meet personal needs. There may be a tendency to negotiate directly for a rule change when rules are clearly set. At times, the child may ignore rules and therefore avoid them entirely.

Limitations in Social Decision Making

The following list presents the common problems found in the area of social decision making.

Recognize the Social Problem or Situation The child may have deficits in any of the following areas: becoming so engrossed in a situation that he or she fails to notice the social dynamic; the ability to notice social difficulty, but unable to ascertain the relevant social cues; an inability to identify a problem or issue; and a lack of motivation to address a solution.

Generate Options The child fails to understand the viewpoints and emotions of others, discounts options proposed by others, impulsively produces irrelevant or tangential options, or generates too few or too many options.

Consider Consequences of Options The child fails to engage in this step of decision making and immediately jumps to implementation of a strategy. He or she finds it difficult to understand the concept of consequences or outcomes of choices and is unable to rank them according to desirability.

Choose the Best Option The child makes choices based on popularity, egotism, impulsivity, or familiarity. The child is unable to determine the means of deciding the preferred strategy or cannot make a decision.

Implement Strategy The child may execute a faulty or inadequate implementation of a solution. The child may give up on the strategy too quickly or jump between strategies.

Evaluate Results The child may fail to evaluate the results, misinterpret the outcome, or attribute incorrect reasons for the success or failure of the strategy. The child may also ignore results or consequences, and may not generalize the knowledge gained from the results of one situation to future situations.

Common Behavioral Profiles

This chapter presents descriptions of nine common behavioral profiles of children with social skills difficulties. Identification of these characteristic behaviors is based on years of clinical experience working with a broad array of children; these are profiles and not discrete descriptors of a particular child. Each profile is a composite of numerous children who exhibit similarities in conduct, life histories, and psychological makeup. Often, the behavior of a specific child will reflect elements from more than one profile.

There are four primary ways that these behavioral profiles can be used in practice. First, these profiles enhance our general understanding of the common characteristics of diverse children with problems in the social arena. Second, the profiles can help to determine the service needs of the child, whether targeting the social deficit or addressing related difficulties. Third, the profiles cluster a child's behavior into a clinical picture that assists the assessment and goal-setting process. And fourth, they may aid in determining effective intervention strategies. Applications to assessment and intervention appear in later sections of the book. These profiles should be used for reference only, and not be misused to foster stereotypic thinking about children.

Behavioral Profiles

Controlling

Children who exhibit controlling behavior are typically rigid and inflexible. They try to be in charge of everything in order to protect their fragile egos. If they produce an idea, these children can be cooperative. However, if someone else generates an idea, they are generally uncooperative. Controlling children express control in a number of ways, including using charm to win other people to their perspective and to take charge, refusing to cooperate in order to win a power struggle, and insisting on having things their own way. The behavior of these children exhibits a Jekyll and Hyde quality, in that they vacillate between periods of being "good" and "bad."

Children with controlling behavioral profiles are often bright, socially savvy, and effective in reading people. However, all of these admirable qualities can be turned around and used to intimidate others. Social skills may be part of their repertoire but may not be used, or used only in a restricted manner. When these children are younger, their behavior appears to be generally difficult and poorly regulated. They develop a more defined behavioral pattern around 8 years of age and older.

Defiant

Children who exhibit defiant behavior may be disrespectful and argumentative and may demonstrate this behavior to parents, teachers, and peers with little emotional investment. These children say that they do not care about others; therefore, it makes little difference to them what others think and whether feelings are hurt. At times, some of these children can be mean-spirited, cruel, and occasionally physically abusive. Through posture and language they say, "I won't! No! You can't make me!" and "It's my way or the highway!" Children with this profile typically push boundaries to the limit.

Some key reasons for defiance include seeking attention, covering up emotional vulnerabilities, and avoiding risks of rejection. The pain from social isolation and low self-esteem is so acute in some children that they compensate with defiant behavior. This defiance may be complicated by learning disabilities, hyperactivity, and competition with parents. Timely identification and intervention are critical to prevent a full picture of defiance from emerging. Early problems of inattention with hyperactivity can lead to defiant behavior in some children. This behavioral pattern can later develop into oppositional defiant disorder.

Limit Testing

Children who engage in active limit-testing behavior may want to please but appear to have a need to push everyone's buttons and bend the rules. Their behavior is often provocative in that it challenges ("Why do I need to stop playing now?") or ignores others (such as actively tuning out requests). Adults and peers find they have to repeat instructions, directions, and requests. Examples of limit testing are numerous. These children may monopolize the discussion at circle time despite reminders to give others a turn; they may pose challenging questions in response to every situation; they may habitually attempt to change the rules of the game or activity so that they can win or get what they want.

Children who exhibit limit-testing behavior may act in this manner for a variety of reasons. They may test limits in order to gather information about the world to make sure that it is stable and predictable. They may be unable to read the nonverbal signals of peers and adults, or they may overfocus on what they want or are doing and cannot shift attention and be adaptable. They may enjoy the emotional excitement of instigating frustration in others or simply enjoy the power of having the last word. The limit-testing behavioral profile is not typically as extreme as the behavior of children with issues related to control or defiance.

Bullying

Children who exhibit bullying behavior may engage in activity that causes physical or emotional harm to others. These children are into power and may be willfully malicious and mean-spirited; behaviors may range from teasing to verbal and physical intimidation. While these children may bully anyone who is available, at times there may be a pecking order in which the bully targets one particular victim. The abusive behavior is often seen in public places such as the playground and school bus but can also occur in private where there are no witnesses.

Some parents and teachers may covertly allow the bullying to occur. Adults may feel that the victim has done something to provoke the bullying and therefore it is justified. Or they believe that the children need to work it out; that only by participating in the process will the victim learn to stand up for him- or herself. Bullying is never justified and should not be tolerated. The victim feels vulnerable and unsafe, and the bully is reinforced to feel that physical power and emotional intimidation are legitimate means for managing relationships. Both children come to believe that the community where the behavior occurs condones it; the bully feels there will be no sanctions and the victim believes there will be no relief. Both perspectives need to be changed.

Discounting

Children who exhibit discounting behavior disregard the comments of others and invalidate their statements. Their inappropriate behavior is commonly seen when interacting with parents, teachers and peers alike. These children are often bright and precocious with language, and they tend to dominate the conversation. This behavioral pattern is often seen in children with attention deficit hyperactivity disorder. The following examples typify their behavior.

- The parent says that it is dark outside. The child replies, "But in Rangoon it is daylight!"
- One child exclaims with pride that she has five Beanie Babies®. The discounting child retorts, "I have 10, and you can't get them anymore!"
- A child shows a beautiful long-stem rose to her friends. The discounting child declares, "That's not a rose. It's a bud!"

Typically, children with this profile are not malicious but they feel the need to be always right. They are overfocused on facts and information, ignoring or not noticing that the conversation has become pedantic. These children have difficulty in making small talk and knowing how to hang out and shoot the breeze. They are most comfortable in instrumental exchanges and avoid social-emotional interactions. Unaware of the impact of their behavior on others, these children may not understand the angry and hurt feelings generated by their put-downs. Likewise, they may not be aware of others' perception of them, as other children may see the discounter as an annoying, frustrating jerk. His or her interest in sharing concrete, factual information overrides any concern with the personal response of the listener. This lack of social perception often leads to the discounting child being interpreted as an insensitive bore.

Egocentric

Children who exhibit egocentric behavior must have things their own way or they withdraw from the activity. Egocentric children tend to be narcissistic and unable to recognize or accept the perspective of others, that is, they have difficulty de-centering from their own motives and preferences. Typical egocentric thinking and behavior reflect a certain inflexibility; new information is not easily incorporated to alter an original view. These children see the world through a narrow perspective, hold to their viewpoint, and are unaware of the negative reactions of others. They frequently act immature for their ages and therefore their behavior is considered developmentally inappropriate.

Egocentric children often demonstrate self-centered behavior. For example, Leroy was in a classroom during the social studies lesson. He was adamant to be the first to share his homework, to be the first to practice map reading, to be the first to hand out materials, to be the first to choose the next study topic, to be the first at everything. In Leroy's case it was always "me, me, me." Trudy demonstrated a different pattern. If she had not personally experienced an event, she could not conceive of it as being possible. For instance, when Davy said that a Japanese friend was coming to play at his house, Trudy protested, "That's not possible; you don't speak Japanese!" Davy explained that the friend was American. Trudy could not accept the statement because she had never seen a Japanese-American child. In another instance, Roger became very upset and stopped a dodgeball game because he felt that his peers were picking on him. To Roger, every throw of the ball was aimed at him; he could not de-center and recognize that everyone was a shared target.

An egocentric child is often considered a brat. Stuck in an early developmental progression from egotism to altruism, some egocentric children may have the intellectual understanding of the perspective of others but are unable to act upon it. In general, egotistical behavior becomes worse when the child is under stress, experiences competition, or feels ill. Other adults sometimes view parents of egocentric children judgmentally, seeing the parents as indulgent and spoiling the child; while this may be true in some cases, it is not typical.

Low Self-Esteem

Children with low self-esteem are commonly seen in two patterns: internalizing and externalizing. The more frequent pattern involves children who internalize their emotions. They are self-deprecating, cannot accept positive feedback, and criticize themselves even though no one else does. They avoid risk taking and play it safe because of a lack of self-confidence. Both expecting and fearing failure, these children may lack persistence in tasks and give up readily, or they may become perfectionists and work diligently to avoid the possibility of failure.

Internalizing children with low self-esteem are overly sensitive to stress and may be hyper-alert to criticism and feedback. Their physical demeanor is commonly withdrawn and inhibited. As a result, these children typically possess a restricted social world because they tend to prefer interacting with non-threatening children. Dodging shame and embarrassment at all costs, these children do not speak up on their own behalf and practice conformity. They shun anger, confrontation, and disagreement so that they do not stick out.

The second and less common pattern of low self-esteem involves children who compensate by externalizing emotions. These children brag, show off, need to win, and seek attention. They collect a diversity of experiences and accomplishments in order to feel good about themselves. Yet regardless of their achievements, these children continue to feel inadequate. At times they may engage in discounting in order to enhance their sense of self. A case in point is Pedro, whose low self-esteem was related to his short stature. Pedro complained to his mother, "None of the boys like me, and they make fun of my size." Pedro had developed a personality pattern to compensate for his painful feelings; he was loud, aggressive, and demeaning. This externalizing behavior failed to soothe his pain and also reinforced the social withdrawal of his peers.

Language Difficulty

Children with language delays and/or disorders are seen in a diversity of clinical manifestations because of the different types of speech and language deficits. Problems in communication are very common in children with poor social skills. These children are wary and apprehensive about social situations, often worrying that they will not understand what is going on or be able to respond verbally. Some children respond to their communication challenges by becoming shy and withdrawn, while others may become frustrated and aggressive.

These children may have a delay in receptive skills, expressive skills, or both. Difficulties often are seen in conversations, play negotiations, and turn taking. Because they are working so hard to comprehend and then construct sentences, children with language difficulties fail to maintain the pace of back and forth exchanges. The social ramifications are significant but sometimes perplexing. The language problem may be subtle and not apparent in some children, yet other children may look foolish due to their language difficulties. In both cases, these children can become socially self-conscious, and adults and peers may not seek their ideas or take them seriously.

Tina is an example of a child with numerous pragmatic, discourse, and language difficulties that interfere with her development of friendships. During a recent social competence group that she attended at school under the direction of an occupational therapist, Tina demonstrated a number of these problems. Her communicative capabilities varied based upon the activity she was participating in and the interaction demanded. In the beginning of the session she stated, "I went to my Mommy and Daddy's wedding," an example of word substitution because she meant to say "anniversary party." At another time, Tina said, "That is funny," when she meant to respond to the speaker's comments by saying, "Was that funny?" In this case, Tina was using a declarative sentence when she meant to ask a question. Later, she described to her peers in a very animated way the contents of a book about Olympic ice skaters. However, she had failed to introduce the book prior to the discourse on its content, leaving the group members somewhat bewildered about why she was sharing the information. Furthermore, Tina was unable to transition from the topic of her book to the group's next topic of interest; she could not break her monologue as the conversation shifted to something else, and repeatedly said, "I'm not finished talking!"

Tyrone is another example of a child whose language limitations interfered with his social competence. He has some functional communication skills when not rushed, and the interaction is concrete and structured. However, if the conversation becomes abstract or fast paced, his problems in auditory processing and receptive language become apparent, and occasionally, he reacts by acting out or withdrawing. The issue of speed of conversation was evident recently, when Tyrone was in the front yard with children from the neighborhood. The other children blurted out the rules for the proposed game and immediately started playing. Tyrone was unable to understand the plan; consequently, he proceeded to play with the rules as he assumed them to be, but was in fact making up new ones. The result was a social catastrophe.

Other examples of Tyrone's identified auditory processing deficit are less obvious. A teacher recently asked him to "Go file the cards." Tyrone was startled by the direction because he heard, "Go fire the cards." He said in a loud voice, "Go fire the cards?" which provoked laughter by the other children because Tyrone appeared to be playing the clown. This example illustrates how an auditory processing problem may contribute to a child developing a reputation as a misbehaving social misfit.

Yet another example occurred when Tyrone was at a family dinner at which spaghetti was served. One of the adults, intending to be humorous, began speaking with a mock Italian accent, and several others joined in the exchange. Tyrone became extremely upset, running to each participant in the dialogue and screaming, "Don't talk that way!" Although the boy appeared to be strange, controlling, and bossy, in reality Tyrone was unnerved by hearing familiar language spoken in such an odd way; he became anxious because he could not understand what was said and felt socially isolated.

Scared

Children who exhibit scared behavior are often shy, timid, and withdrawn. These children do not take risks and are often quiet, exhibit low energy levels, and tend to engage in solitary play. They are usually on the fringes of the social world with very few or no friends. Such children often experience underlying anxiety that reinforces the tendency to remain apart. Scared children are an easy target for bullies and victimization, because they are frequently nonassertive and do not stand up for themselves.

There are a number of factors that may contribute to such behavior. Some children have delays in play skills or limitations in cognition or language. Any of these factors can lead a child to feel overwhelmed by environmental demands that are perceived as too much—too loud, too intrusive, or too intense. Other children have temperamental or neurological vulnerabilities that can foster a frightened style. Some are born constitutionally shy or inhibited in their temperamental make-up. Others may be hypersensitive to stimulation such as touch, sights, sounds, and movement. Such children have a low tolerance for social engagement.

Profiles in Context

These behavioral profiles can help the practitioner to synthesize diverse information about a child into common themes, and to organize thoughts for clinical problem solving based on a more complete picture of the child. Of course, the profiles cannot be seen outside of an environmental context, as behaviors are very much shaped and molded through transactions with the environment. Nor do these behavioral profiles reflect inherent, unchanging characteristics of the child; rather they show a child's tendencies to act in certain ways depending on the social context. A child is not defiant, controlling, or bullying at all times; instead, the emergence of certain behaviors is related to factors of the setting including the number and type of children, the presence or absence of adults, the amount of structure in an environment, the nature of an activity, resemblance to past experiences, and the emotional tone of the moment. The profiles can only be understood in the context of interacting with the social and physical environment.

Dana, a very bright child with a diagnosis of attention deficit disorder, exemplifies the complexity of these children. Her behavioral profile was controlling and defiant, characterized by questioning authority and talking back. However, she acted in this way when she was anxious and stressed. During a social competence group, the children were playing in a relay race. Dana became nervous, loud, and demanding under this competitive environment. Later in the session the children played with familiar board games. At this point she noticed that Jay had become upset because his suggestions were being ignored; he had withdrawn and was sulking in the corner of the room. Dana said to an adult, "Jay is upset. Can I go talk to him?" When the practitioner suggested that Dana go and sit with Jay, she joined him and quietly engaged in talk that comforted him. This overture was profoundly meaningful to Jay, and Dana exhibited prosocial skills that were totally unexpected by the adult. In this case, the social environment fostered the emergence of Dana's best behavior.

Assessment

Assessment of Social Competence

Assessment of social competence is individualized and is based on the presenting needs of the child and family. The conceptual framework provides a structure for the information to be gathered; that is, the practitioner wants to acquire an appreciation of the child's social perspective taking (or level of egocentricity) and the child's purposes of interaction (instrumental versus social emotional). Data is also gathered on the components of social competence: social and play behavior, self-regulation, communication, prosocial skills, and social decision making. Formal and informal ways of collecting this information will be described.

This chapter presents a discussion of both the assessment of social perspective taking and the purposes of interaction, and then a case is made for the distinction between acquisition and performance deficits during the assessment process. Five methods for gathering data about a child's social competence components are described and sample assessment protocols are provided to illustrate the creation of unique assessment formats for different work settings. The importance of assessing a child within the context of his or her environment is emphasized, as social inadequacy may not be due to a problem within the child but rather to an environment that is excessively stressful or demanding.

Social Perspective Taking

Level of egocentricity is determined by assessing the child's degree of social perspective taking. A child's developmental status evolves from a primitive stage of being unable to distinguish his or her own perspective from others toward an awareness of reciprocal perspectives, then mutual perspectives, and finally a societal viewpoint. A movement away from narcissism toward altruism suggests an understanding of social norms and rules and the child's propensity to follow them.

Many behavioral profiles of children with poor social skills illustrate problems in perspective taking. The egocentric child is by definition self-centered and unable to accept the viewpoint of others; the controlling child is inflexible, rigid, and unable to cooperate with others; the defiant child does not care about others or their feelings; the limit testing child over focuses on what he wants and cannot adaptively shift his attention; and the bullying child engages in physical and emotional harm to others because he disregards rules of social behavior. Each of these behavioral profiles exhibits arrested development in their capacity to understand and respect the points of view of others.

A parent interview is an effective method for assessing the child's social perspective taking. The parents often present the child's inability to see the perspective of another person as a primary concern, and may express it in a variety of ways: "He always has to do things his way" is a common theme, as is "Things go well with a friend as long as the other child does what my son wants," and "My child is always arguing with her siblings and others." These types of comments may suggest an inability to consider and adopt the ideas of others.

Purpose of Interactions

A practitioner can best assess the child's use of interactions by listening to how the child talks. Direct observation will reveal whether the child demonstrates social-emotional interactions such as sharing affection, chatting, and shooting the breeze. These interactions express emotions. In contrast instrumental interactions are designed to share information or a tangible product. The adult listens for interactions regarding the performance of tasks and the achievement of concrete goals.

The practitioner must assess these four relevant issues:

1. Is the child able to go from simple to complex interaction statements? For example, some children have very limited social-emotional interactions such as "Hello, how are you?" and are unable to expand interaction to a deeper level.

2. Does the child inappropriately substitute one type of interaction for another? For instance, a child who wishes to bond with a schoolmate may talk in detail about a common homework assignment (an instrumental interaction rather than a social-emotional one), and the classmate may rebuff his efforts as annoying and repetitious.

3. Does the child move fluidly between the use of social-emotional and instrumental interactions? Ideally, there is a balance between the two forms of interaction as well as an ability to blend them in conversation.

4. Are there certain contexts or circumstances in which the child is unable to demonstrate both social-emotional and instrumental interactions? For example, is the child able to use both types of interactions under conditions of developmentally appropriate stress, anxiety or demand? Some children may rely on scripts employing primarily instrumental interactions as a vehicle for gradually learning more social-emotional content.

Acquisition Versus Performance Deficit

During the assessment process the practitioner must make a distinction between two types of difficulties in social behavior (Gresham & Elliott, 1990). An acquisition or skill deficit occurs when the child has not learned the cognitive, communicative, or behavioral skills needed to succeed in social exchanges, while the child with a performance deficit has the necessary skills but does not use them due to some interfering factor. This distinction is important because a child may initially appear socially inept due to a lack of necessary abilities, when in reality the child's skills are masked by such factors as anxiety or depression. Gresham and Elliot (1990) divide the deficits further regarding the presence or absence of problem behaviors.

The child with an acquisition deficit may not have acquired social skills due to specific developmental disorders or delays, such as physical impairment, language impairment, or poor opportunities for learning. For example, minimal skills in peer play may be due to the isolating circumstances of life in the inner city or in some rural regions.

The child with a performance deficit has the necessary social skills but does not always use them at acceptable levels or at appropriate times. For some children, social skills are not mastered or fully retained due to lack of practice; consequently, under the demands and stress of social encounters, these skills are no longer available to them. For instance, a child's verbal fluency and social give-and-take may be temporarily lost. The impact of performance anxiety when interacting with peers cannot be underestimated. There is a constant tension of wanting to be admired, accepted, and validated as a person and member of the group. The child may also have an emotional response or specific problem behavior that interferes with the ability to use acquired skills effectively; examples include fear, impulsivity, hyperactivity, and distractibility. A case in point is Bobby Ray, who is interactive and compassionate with other children when he does not have a particular agenda to pursue. However, under the stress of getting his popularity needs met, Bobby Ray assumes an arrogant and condescending attitude toward peers, automatically assuming this posture due to the intensity of his emotional involvement in pursuing success.

During an assessment, the practitioner needs to directly examine whether the child has a deficit in acquiring social skills or a deficit in performance. This distinction can be made by observing the child over time and in a variety of social arenas, evaluating which social skills are available, emerging, constricted, missing, or present under certain circumstances but not in others. For instance, Kareem would not share his knowledge of the rules of a board game when he was playing it at a cousin's party, appearing self-conscious and allowing the children to misinterpret the rules. In contrast, when playing with his neighborhood friends, Kareem was very vocal about how the game should be played. This difference in behavior is characteristic of a performance deficit. When he is self-conscious or anxious, Kareem becomes very passive and fails to display any assertive behaviors. Indeed, Kareem fails to show leadership in any setting, including school, except for the narrow focus of this familiar group of children.

Data Collection

Various methods exist for gathering data about the child's strengths and vulnerabilities as related to the components of social competence in the conceptual framework. There is no ideal protocol for this assessment process; the practitioner must choose the most meaningful methods of data collection given his or her roles and expertise, the children being served, and the resources of the provider agency. To acquire a comprehensive view of each child, at least three of the methods of data collection reviewed later in this chapter should be used. The initial assessment should gather enough information to allow the practitioner to set relevant goals and preliminary strategies for intervention. Sequential assessment over time is essential for refining the practitioner's understanding of the child, which enables more targeted intervention planning (see Elksnin and Elksnin [1998] for a survey of assessment approaches).

Information acquired during an initial assessment is often tentative and somewhat limited in scope. For some children with marked difficulties, first impressions may be valid. However, for children with more subtle and complex needs, understanding their social reality takes time, astute observation in a variety of contexts, and more interpersonal contact such as child-practitioner interaction. Over time, behaviors may emerge that were not present during the initial evaluation. Some children are so self-protective or resistant to disclosure that they reveal their troubling behavior only over time. Therefore, premature or hasty clinical judgments must be avoided.

There are many different methods for gathering information about a child's social functioning. These methods include rating scales and questionnaires, interviews, behavioral observation, problem-solving tasks, and sociometric techniques, all of which can be used to assess the components of social competence highlighted in the conceptual framework. Depending on the child, a rather in-depth assessment may be made in one or two areas, while the rest may receive only a generic screening. For instance, a child with a major language problem may receive a complete assessment of his or her communication related to social performance and a quick screening of self-regulation. Typically, an assessment protocol needs to use at least three methods of data collection.

Rating Scales and Questionnaires

Parents, teachers, other caregivers, and the child are sources of valuable information, and a number of standardized instruments can be used to gather information on a child's social abilities. A sample of four rating scales and questionnaires are presented in this discussion.

The *Social Skills Rating System* (SSRS; Gresham & Elliott, 1990), noteworthy because of its psychometric validation, assesses prosocial skills, problem behaviors, and academic competence. Teacher and parent forms are available for preschool, kindergarten through grade 6, and grades 7–12; student self-rating forms are available for grades 3–6 and grades 7–12. By using this instrument, the practitioner can gather data from a number of perspectives, including that of the child, the parents, the teacher, and possibly those of other relevant professionals. This composite data collection enables the practitioner to have a more complete picture of the child's social world and also from the unique vantage point of each respondent.

The five subscales of the SSRS address the area of prosocial skills, namely cooperation, assertion, responsibility, empathy, and self-control. The rater records the frequency and the importance of each item for the child's successful social performance. There are also three subscales related to self-regulation that address the area of problem behaviors: externalizing problems such as poor control of temper, arguing, and aggression; internalizing problems such as poor self-esteem, sadness, and anxiety; and hyperactivity such as impulsivity and fidgeting.

The teacher surveys at the elementary and secondary levels also provide an overview of the child's academic competence. This SSRS generic appraisal of the child's classroom performance identifies the extent to which deficits in social skills and problem behaviors influence academic achievement. The instrument focuses on one major context in which the child has to succeed, that of the school setting. The SSRS has the benefit of national norms that are standardized on more than 4,000 children with and without disabilities.

The *Self-Awareness Assessment* (Dorman, 1999) is a means of gathering data about older children's perceptions of their social adequacy. Used with children ages 9 though 12, the instrument has 10 items that reflect positive social statements such as "I can make friends easily" (see Appendix A.1). The child responds to the items using a 3-point Likert scale regarding the level of agreement with the statement; that is, choosing *Rarely, Sometimes,* or *Often.* The instrument is tabulated by clustering all of the *Often* statements together to indicate the child's social strengths, which are then used to create therapeutic strategies to address the vulnerabilities. Items that receive *Rarely* responses are the child's self-assessed areas of weakness and become the targets of intervention. The practitioner needs to talk with the child about each item that was difficult, and the examples generated provide concrete objectives to be addressed in intervention.

The *Child and Family Profile* (Williamson, 2000), presented in Appendix A.2, addresses health history, concerns of the family, parenting issues, and the social and play behavior of the child. Information gathered in this questionnaire can serve as the basis for discussion with the parents and for determining further assessment activities.

The *Identification of Social Difficulties Questionnaire* (Dorman & Williamson, 2000), presented in Appendix A.3, is also useful for screening purposes. This form, completed by parents regarding their perception of the child's social abilities, asks direct questions about social and play behavior, self-regulation, prosocial skills, communication, and social decision making; the parents answer each question using a 3-point Likert scale.

Interviews

Interviews with parents, the child, and other involved individuals such as teachers can either be a part of the initial assessment or conducted sequentially over time. Each individual can be interviewed separately, or a combined session with the parents and child together may be useful. An interview may be started with both parents and child, and followed by private time with each. The best interviews are informal and conversational in tone so that all participants are comfortable.

The interview method provides a wealth of positive benefits. A well-planned and successful interview is the beginning of an alliance with the parent and the child, establishing a foundation for a collaborative relationship. New assessment information is gathered that may not have been revealed in any questionnaire, and the collected data can be clarified through a shared exchange. Questions can be targeted to address the child's social and play behavior, self-regulation, prosocial skills, communication, and social decision making. The interview provides an opportunity to observe the social behaviors and interactions of the parent and child. Three examples of these interactions come to mind:

1. The practitioner can observe if the adult is serving as a desired social model for the child, as some parents unwittingly demonstrate negative behaviors such as frequent interrupting.

2. The practitioner can observe the degree of respect between the parent and child. It is significant if parents undercut their children by discounting their perspectives and opinions.

3. The interview can reveal whether there is agreement between the child and parent concerning the present situation, as they can agree or disagree that a social problem exists. On occasion, when an outside party is responsible for the referral, family members may not recognize a difficulty or the need for help.

An open interview provides the possibility for the parents to learn about the therapeutic program and to ask questions. Through this dialogue, the preliminary goals and priorities of intervention can be developed.

The interview method does have limitations. Interviews tend to be time-consuming, and the practitioner may develop a distorted perspective if shared information is only partially complete. Additional data sources such as interviews with or questionnaires completed by the classroom teacher or **school psychologist** offer insightful information. Also, conducting an effective interview is a **sophisticated** skill requiring training and experience. The interviewer must be able to establish a trusting, respectful relationship with the interviewee as subjects may be discussed that are sensitive in nature and may cause the child, parent, or practitioner to become uncomfortable or defensive. The interviewer needs to be able to work through sensitive subject matter in active cooperation with the participants, and by the end of the session, critical items need to have been addressed. An interview should conclude on a positive note. Table 8.1 provides sample questions that can be incorporated into an interview with parents.

Table 8.1
Sample Interview Questions to Parents

- What prompted you to come here?
- How long have you been concerned?
- Has your child received professional help for these issues in the past?
- Can you describe the various behaviors you are concerned about?
- Do your child's social difficulties occur at school, at home, or in the community?
- Did your child play with appropriate games and toys while growing up?
- Are there situations that make your child's behavior worse?
- Are there times of the day when things are harder for your child?
- How does homework go? Bedtime? Preparation for school? Formal social events?
- Is your child on medication?
- What do you want to achieve? What are your priorities?

The interview of the child is personalized to reveal an understanding of his or her social world. The sample questions in Table 8.2 are provided as a starting point for the discussion; they should be tailored to fit within the context of a smooth conversation. Generally, questions that are concrete and not emotionally laden should be asked before inquiries about more sensitive social information. For instance, asking about activity preferences in school may elicit free sharing by the child and, therefore, serve as an icebreaker, and the adult is put in the role of empathic listener early in the interview process. Throughout the course of the interview, the adult can ask questions about any component of the child's social performance in the conceptual framework.

Table 8.2
Sample Interview Questions to a Child

- What did your Mom or Dad tell you about coming here today?
- Can you tell me more about that?
- What do you like best about school?
- What do you like least about school?
- Who are your friends at school?
- What do you play at school?
- When you are home on weekends, what do you do?
- Who do you play with on weekends?
- Do you belong to any clubs or participate in any sports?
- Who are your friends in the neighborhood?
- Who invites you over to play? What do you do? Do you get invited back?
- Do you invite anyone over? What do you do? If that does not work, what else do you do?

Behavioral Observation

A key aspect of the assessment process is to observe the child in a variety of social situations such as the classroom, on the playground, and in the cafeteria. The child's social competence may vary dramatically depending upon the characteristics of each social context. For example, the teacher was concerned that Tabitha was excessively shy and emotionally constrained because of her performance in the classroom. However, further observation revealed that Tabitha was rather outgoing in the hallway and at recess, and her social constriction in the classroom appeared to be a reflection of her general anxiety about academic performance. Thus, naturalistic observation in different contexts gives the most accurate picture of a child's social functioning.

Social skills do not occur in a vacuum but in transactions among the child, other people, and the physical environment. Therefore the practitioner must assess the characteristics of the social setting and their influence on the child's interactive competence. A child may be socially adept in one context and inadequate in another. A child may relate to a teacher in one way in the classroom and another way during an informal field trip; likewise, the child may behave in a certain way with his parents' adult friends while carpooling and another way at a neighborhood cookout. Similarly, the child may react differently when playing with children who are behaving as opposed to playing with the same children when they are misbehaving. Or the child may get along fine in a small group when there is structure but argue and fight when structure is missing. The assessment delineates these qualitative differences in performance as they relate to the environmental context.

An assessment structure helps to guide one's observation of children. Observational tools used during free play, informal social interaction, or structured activities can assist the practitioner in focusing on salient aspects of the child's social behavior. Appendix A.4 presents the *Teacher Impression Scale* developed by Odom and McConnell (1993). This rating scale is used for direct observation of a child during a 5-minute segment, and this procedure is repeated three to four times over a 2-week period. The teacher then determines whether the child needs intervention by examining individual item scores and overall summary scores. The *Teacher Impression Scale* was developed as an assessment tool to accompany a published curriculum, and we have adapted its use as an informal observation instrument to form a general impression about the prosocial skills of the child as part of a screening or initial evaluation.

Another observation instrument that helps the practitioner focus on the components of social competence, as we define them in this text, is the *Components of Social Competence Observation Scale* (Williamson 2000), presented in Appendix A.5. The practitioner rates each component; that is, social and play behavior, self-regulation, communication, and social decision making (prosocial skills are not directly emphasized in this instrument because of the numerous tools available to address this domain). The scale breaks down the rated areas into discrete, observable behaviors that are critical for social proficiency. Preferably, the scale is completed after observing the child a number of times.

Many practitioners do not have the option of observing the child in a variety of contexts such as the school, the home, and the neighborhood; consequently, it may be helpful to design a *structured play observation* within the context of your assessment process. Because the practitioner is addressing the child's social behavior, direct observation of social interaction is useful. You may want to incorporate a small group play session in the evaluation. Three to four children who are candidates for social competence intervention can be scheduled at the same time, and in this way the children can be observed interacting with each other during the assessment. Approximately 20–40 minutes can be devoted to various activities that invite social engagement. For example, the session can begin with a warm-up activity for getting to know each other, followed by a gross motor task such as an obstacle course or modified ball game, and a wrap-up activity which provides an opportunity for the children to feel successful and motivated for continued involvement with the practitioner.

The *Components of Social Competence Observation Scale* can be used to record the social performance of the children, or a practitioner may choose to develop an original checklist that targets behaviors of particular concern to a unique population or setting. The practitioner can also record the child's behavior through anecdotal logs and frequency counts of targeted skills. Recording the antecedents and consequences of target behaviors to determine the dynamics of an interaction is especially valuable. Videotaping short segments of the child's behavior in different contexts is another way to document behavioral observations. This approach has the advantage of a concrete behavioral record that can be reviewed numerous times, and the video can be taped by an aide or volunteer so that the professional's time demands are more flexible.

With experience, the practitioner develops an automatic thinking process for clinical observation and reasoning. Regardless of the system used, the following items reflect the five components of social competence described in the conceptual framework and may be highlighted in the observation.

Attention	Degree of Participation	Following Directions
Impulsivity	Awareness of Others	Accepting Responsibility
Emotional Reactivity	Initiation of Conversation	Prosocial Skills
Eye Contact	Relevance of Conversation	Play Repertoire
Body Language	Maintains Conversation	Personality

Problem-Solving Tasks

As one aspect of the assessment process, the practitioner can engage the child in solving social problems. A social dilemma can be presented verbally as a vignette or script, through picture cards, or as a role-play. The child is then asked to describe the solution to the problem or to act it out. The practitioner can evaluate any of the components of the child's social competence with this method. For example, the practitioner can provide an example that says, "You want to play with Johnny, and he says, 'No!' What would you say? What would you do?" In the use of picture cards one can have a picture of two children watching a television show with one of the children changing the channel. The other child clearly wants to continue watching the initial TV show. The practitioner inquires, "What should he say? What should he do? If that plan does not work, what else can he do?" A role-play could be introduced between the child and practitioner or with peers; a sample scenario to be acted out could focus on a child being teased by a bully due to his style of dress. The adult then says, "Now we are going to pretend that we are the people in this scene. Act out what you would say and do if you were that child!" and the role-play is initiated.

These problem-solving tasks have the benefit of assessing social reasoning and decision-making skills and also help to evaluate the level of the child's egocentricity by examining the capacity to take another's role and point of view. The child's responses can be followed up with further questioning to tap the breadth and depth of his or her thinking. However, there is a real limitation in using this method. Some children can provide elaborate responses about what should be done, but in their personal lives they do not demonstrate the competence evident in their thinking; they can say it but not do it. Other children do not have the verbal or reflective skills to describe their thinking but are able to perform adequately; they cannot say it but they can do it. For instance, Harvey cannot describe what he thinks due to a language deficit. During the assessment he did poorly on the vignette, but during the naturalistic play observation he proved to have adequate social and play skills. Given the limitations in validity of the social decision-making tasks, it is best to not emphasize them in the assessment process.

Sociometric Techniques

A child's social status and acceptance can be determined either by peer nomination sociometrics or peer rating scales. In the peer nomination method a group of children are asked to list a certain number of classmates regarding a specific criterion. To illustrate, the children may be asked to nominate the classmates they would most want to play with or have over after school. Negative nominations can also be requested such as, "Which children would you least like to play with?" This procedure provides a ranking or diagram of the social hierarchy of the group on the particular trait.

In the peer rating scale each child rates every peer in a group according to prescribed criteria. For instance, they would rate every child according to the degree of preference on a Likert scale regarding desirability as a work partner. A child's score is the average of ratings received and can be compared with the scores of other children in the group.

Some practitioners feel uncomfortable using sociometric techniques that invite children to socially compare and rate other children, due to fear that this procedure can promote further stigmatization. Another drawback of the peer nomination method is that the practitioner does not know why the choices are made; that is, why particular children are liked or disliked. In addition, information is lacking about children who are not nominated and tend to be neglected. The peer rating scale tends to be more reliable and sensitive to change than the peer nomination approach and also tends to have better predictive validity.

Some children may make real improvements in their social skills because of intervention or maturation, but this positive change may not result in a corresponding improvement on a sociometric measure. Children tend to hold fast to initial impressions and labels of a peer, and may be resistant to forming a new opinion. Given this reality, child study teams should consider classroom placement and composition very carefully based on this information. A child can be tyrannized by an old label that follows him or her from school year to school year.

Sample Assessment Protocols

Various means for gathering information about a child's social functioning can be used in any combination based on the presenting needs of the children and the intervention setting. To illustrate, we are going to examine four situations in which assessment procedures may be used: an outpatient facility, two school-based programs, and a community-based program. In each scenario, the practitioner has designed an assessment protocol tailored to the unique features of the environment.

Outpatient Facility

This assessment model was created for an outpatient rehabilitation facility and therapy private practice. Both settings conducted social competence groups on a regular basis after school and received referrals directly from parents and practitioners in the community. In contrast to a school-based situation in which the children are familiar to the practitioner, in these settings the children are not known before the assessment process.

- **Telephone interview with parents.** The practitioner talks with the parents about their concerns, the child's social status, and the child's potential for intervention. A description of the assessment process is given, and program options are discussed. Pertinent aspects of the child's record are requested such as social skills questionnaires and speech therapy, psychology, and educational reports. This phone conversation is the first step of intervention and is absolutely crucial in beginning the family alliance, as the family is the richest source of information and insight about the child.

- **Record review.** The practitioner reviews all of the materials that have been sent as well as the notes from the initial phone conversation and develops an impression of the child's relevant social history, strengths, and vulnerabilities in the social arena as well as the major presenting problems.

- **Interview.** The interview is the first direct contact of the practitioner and the family. Typically, the practitioner interviews the child and family together, but the parents or the child may be interviewed independently before the end of the session. At this time the practitioner makes recommendations for placement and shares preliminary thoughts on intervention goals.

- **Setting goals and objectives.** After two to three intervention sessions in the group program, the practitioner confirms the specific goals and objectives for the intervention period with the parents. Findings and functional outcomes are documented.

School-Based Practitioner

A practitioner who is not based in the classroom, such as an occupational therapist, speech pathologist, social worker, or psychologist, conducts the assessment. The child is brought to the practitioner's attention by the classroom teacher or a member of the child study team that initiates the assessment process.

- **Consultation with the teacher.** The practitioner interviews the teacher regarding the child's social behavior in the classroom and on the playground.

- **Review record.** The practitioner reviews the relevant psychosocial and educational record in light of the presenting social concerns.

- **Naturalistic observation.** The practitioner observes the child in a variety of contexts in order to get a representative sample of the child's behavior; these settings may include the classroom at different times, the cafeteria, the hallway, the gym, or the playground. Attention focuses on the components of social competence (see Appendix A.5 for an observation scale).

- **Parent interview.** The practitioner talks to the parents in person or over the phone. The discussion targets the parents' concerns, perspectives regarding the child's skills, and priorities for intervention. Any inconsistencies in the child's behavior between home and school are noted. The practitioner should be concerned with social behaviors that lead to success in both the classroom and the community.

- **Determine model of intervention.** Based on the preceding assessment activities, personalized goals and objectives are developed and one or more models of intervention are chosen. At least five models, or combinations, may be considered by the practitioner and other school personnel and written into the child's Individualized Education Plan when indicated.

  1. The practitioner can provide consultation to the teacher and others related to the child's status and ways to promote social integration.

  2. The child can attend a social competence group that is led by the practitioner in a pullout format from the classroom. Children in the regularly scheduled group could be pulled from one or several classrooms.

  3. The child can participate in therapy on an individual basis or in pairs to focus on elements of social competence.

  4. Participation in ongoing special activities can be scheduled, such as afterschool clubs or therapy-run groups on the playground, in the cafeteria, or in the classroom.

  5. The practitioner can work with groups of children within the typical classroom routines.

Classroom-Based Teacher

Teachers have an ideal opportunity to address the social behaviors of the children in their classroom. Because of the frequency and intensity of day-to-day contact, these professionals have the potential of assessing and enhancing the children's social competence.

- **Observation of students.** The teacher can observe the child throughout the day during structured and unstructured activities. A simple observational tool can help guide the teacher's attention; resources include the *Social Skills Rating System* (Gresham & Elliott, 1990) or the *Components of Social Competence Observation Scale* (Williamson, 2000). These insights can be partially confirmed by reviewing report cards regarding the child's behavior.

- **Communication with others.** Discussions with the family regarding the child's social status help to generate collaborative goals for intervention. Input from other school personnel, such as members of the child study team, can provide an interdisciplinary perspective to the action plan.

- **Determine model of intervention.** The teacher has a number of options for providing socially relevant services based on the child's individualized goals and objectives.

  1. The teacher can introduce a social competence program within the classroom curriculum. Specific lessons regarding social skills are offered on a regularly scheduled basis to the class.

  2. The teacher can intervene informally by incorporating social skills training in the moment-to-moment daily interactions with students. For example, the teacher can set standards and expectations for desired social behavior, model the behaviors, coach the children regarding social rules, and provide feedback on their performance.

  3. The teacher can schedule small groups or pairs of children to address social competence. A major intent of this book is to encourage teachers and related service personnel to conduct these social competence groups as a natural ingredient of the classroom curriculum.

Community-Based Programs

There are many community-based programs that can incorporate targeted social competence interventions, including scouts, YMCA programs, 4-H Clubs, youth groups, Little League, and other sports organizations. These programs already have a major emphasis on prosocial skills, altruistic behavior, sportsmanship, and socialization; therefore, adult leaders may choose to incorporate the principles and activities of this book into the general fabric of the program. As a result, all of the participating children would benefit from an enriched environment that enhances social development. In addition, the group leader could be concerned about one or two children who are having difficulty adjusting to the social demands of the program. The leader is motivated to provide special support for these children so that they can be better integrated into the group, and in this case, the assessment would probably be informal and brief. The adult could use a simple observation form to capture the areas of greatest concern as well as areas of social strength. Discussion with the parents helps to confirm whether the leader's perspective regarding the child's social status is shared, and a cooperative approach to the problem can then be generated.

Environmental Context

Social competence is dependent on good fit between the demands of the social and physical environment and the child's resources. An important goal of intervention is to establish a balance between demands on the child and the child's personal resources to meet them. These resources can be categorized as internal (such as the child's beliefs and values, developmental skills, coping style, physical and affective state) and as external(including social support and material and environmental support). Intervention by a parent or practitioner can influence the goodness of fit by modifying the social demand, enhancing coping resources, and providing accurate feedback about the child's social performance. A goodness of fit is not an "all or nothing" phenomenon. It can range on a continuum from a total lack of fit, to a near fit, to a good fit. The demand can be too high, too low, or inconsistent; the resources can be inadequate, absent, or erratic.

Social inadequacy is not always due to a problem in the child. Rather than automatically assuming pathology in the child, the practitioner should examine the entire environmental context to understand what is happening. Too often the behavior of the child is seen as willful and not as a possible reaction to an environmental mismatch. The following vignettes are examples of the environment providing inappropriate demand and stress on a child who is socially intact.

- Matthew is a typically developing boy who at age 6 has the opportunity to play only with older kids in the neighborhood. Because he wants to play, Matthew has to endure frequent teasing for being a "runt" who is unable to "keep up." In response to these taunts, Matthew retreats in tears. In this case, Matthew's social performance looks "immature" only when contrasted with the older children, when in reality, he is socially at age level and demonstrates this when he is playing with his classmates at school.

- A father has a passion for team sports and pushes his son to play in Little League baseball, but his son would rather stay home and play with his neighborhood friends in their clubhouse. The undue pressure to perform causes the child to be challenging to the coach and provocative towards his teammates; these behaviors are not seen when he plays with his neighborhood friends. The poor fit in Little League is due to a mismatch between the child's preferences and the father's personal goals for him to play baseball, and also due to the child's desire to be with a peer group of his choice rather than a group from a nearby community.

- Robby experienced going to the doctor's office as being an environmental stressor. He had a very long wait for his checkup for summer camp, and the setting was noisy, crowded, and congested. Robby felt himself becoming increasingly apprehensive. His older sister, Wilma, came to the rescue as a source of comfort. She distracted him by showing interesting photos in the office magazines; in this case, she was a coping resource for Robby by providing social support. The environment in this situation contained both stressors and resources.

- Jackson is a 4-year-old child with very low muscle tone. His postural control is poor when seated on the floor. As a result, during circle time he tends to lose attention and lean against the closest child, and he becomes distracted and distracting to the group. His focus is on the challenge of maintaining his posture, and therefore social skills are restricted. In contrast, when Jackson is standing or seated at a table, his postural control is better. He is free to use his age appropriate repertoire of social abilities. Thus the physical environment can support the child's social engagement or undermine it.

The properties of the physical environment can determine how socially competent children may be. Children are often more socially skillful in the structure of a classroom than on the playground and in the gymnasium, both of which have minimal structure and large open spaces. This is particularly true for any child who has difficulty organizing play behavior or needs physical boundaries to remain focused. In an unstructured open environment, the child may fall apart, become wild and intrusive, or hug the walls while seeking the peripheral boundaries away from the intimidating center of the play space. In contrast, the same child may be socially engaging in the various learning centers of the classroom and can be a leader in that environment.

Difficulty in dealing with various environments can have a lasting effect on the child. The reputation of children tends to live on even when the children have changed and the reputation is out of date, and peers may interact with the child in habitual ways without acknowledging that the child has socially improved. A child may have made socially significant developmental gains over a summer, as a result of intervention, life experience, or maturation. When school resumes, the child demonstrates an appropriate level of social maturity and no longer behaves in old patterns. Yet his peers treat him the same as they did before the change. In this case, the peers need to shift their perspective of the child to accommodate the new reality.

The assessment of environmental considerations in understanding a child's social competence is crucial, as the environment can set the demand for social engagement and can also serve as a resource to support it. When a child is experiencing social difficulties, the practitioner must identify where the problem is located, whether primarily within the child, within the environment, or in transaction between them. Information can be obtained through observation and interview during the assessment process, and the practitioner should investigate the child's behavior across contexts to have a complete picture.

Goal Setting

Specifically designed goals and objectives are crucial to an individualized approach to intervention and must be based on a review of the child's strengths and weaknesses. Identified areas of vulnerability may become goals for remediation and compensation, while areas of perceived strength are incorporated into intervention strategies for addressing the vulnerabilities. Preferably, the child, parent, and practitioner share responsibility for the generation of intervention goals, because when all parties are in agreement, there is greater likelihood that the goals will be addressed in the varied contexts of the child's life. This chapter discusses the development of individual and group goals and provides examples.

For the purposes of this book, goals are typically outcome oriented and objectively verifiable but may not refer to a specific behavior while objectives, which are means to achieving the goals, are stated in behavioral terminology. A goal may be, "Sunny will use unstructured free play time more purposefully." One objective to achieve this goal may be, "Sunny will play with two toys for 5 minutes each during unstructured free play." Objectives must be observable and demonstrable during the practitioner-child interaction. If a child's goals are to improve sharing and turn taking, the therapeutic and educational setting must provide ample opportunities for these behaviors to be learned and practiced.

The findings from the assessment process are translated into goals and objectives. Depending upon the assessment protocol, data may be gathered from rating scales, questionnaires, interviews, behavioral observations, and problem-solving tasks; this information should reflect input from the child, the parent, and various professionals. Parental preferences and values help to determine goals. The culture of the classroom also influences goal setting. Classrooms vary in their degree of structure, formality, and style of teaching. One classroom may demand advanced social skills because of the heavy use of collaborative learning activities, while another classroom stresses adult-directed instruction and independent learning. The types of goals written for each classroom would be clearly different.

When analyzing the data collected, the practitioner must make distinctions between an acquisition deficit and performance deficit. For an acquisition deficit, the practitioner should attempt to identify why the child has not acquired the target behavior and establishes a goal with that in mind; for instance, a lack of exposure to skill-building opportunities could contribute to the delay in social skills development. For a performance deficit, the practitioner should determine what factors are masking or interfering with the use of learned skills; the child may not perform the skill due to anxiety, boredom, hyper-arousal, or depression. In these circumstances goals would address the interfering factors. During the process of goal setting, a practitioner may decide that a child needs to be referred to an outside professional for further assessment.

Goals must be achievable given the resources of the program, and the practitioner must evaluate formulated goals on several criteria. Can the goals be accomplished in a reasonable length of time? Does the practitioner have the skills as a therapist to address this issue?

Is there sufficient support and cooperation between the school and home to deal with this goal? These types of questions help the practitioner to set goals that are functional and realistic. While goal setting, the practitioner should avoid creating too many goals, as this will result in fragmenting intervention. A few well-chosen goals that address the critical issues are preferred over a longer list. In addition, some goals have a developmental hierarchy and should be addressed in sequence. For example, one might design a goal related to taking the perspective of another as preparation for a more advanced goal of solving conflict situations.

Goals must be based on the priorities shared by the practitioner, parents, and child whenever possible. At times parents, and even the child, have well articulated concerns that they wish to address, such as, "I want my child to stop fighting with other kids" or "I don't have any friends and nobody likes me!" These concerns can be readily translated into goals. However, at other times the child and/or parent may be confused, vague, or ambivalent about participation in a social competence program and unsure about goal setting. They may need help in understanding the need for intervention and assistance in setting meaningful goals, as the following interactions show.

Parent: "His hyperactivity is just like mine was. I made it and so will he."

Practitioner: "Times were different then. The social demands on children are more complex and difficult today. Your child may need assistance in order to succeed the way you have."

Parent: "I recognize that Yi Yin is slow in this stuff, but she'll outgrow it. She is only 5. How important is it anyway?"

Practitioner: "It is important to learn and practice social behaviors at each stage of development rather than trying to catch up later. The early social skills of a 5-year-old serve as the foundation for more advanced skills later."

Parent: "Ryan has lots of interests that are not shared by his peers. He is very bright and they don't understand him."

Practitioner: "You mentioned that Ryan often talks like an adult and at times corrects you. He does this with peers as well, and as a result they tend to ignore and avoid him. Ryan needs to learn how to interact more appropriately with children his own age."

Parent: "Avery is an only child and lives in an area where there are no other children. He likes being alone. His social immaturity is due to his lack of contact with other kids. We don't understand why Avery's teacher is concerned."

Practitioner: "Avery's teacher is concerned that he has no friends. He tends to drift rather aimlessly on the playground and is not sure how to respond to invitations by others. He seems rather sad. Remember, many children have limited opportunities to play with other children in their early years. But by the fourth grade Avery should have had plenty of experience playing with peers. Kids of his age are typically social and enjoy being with each other."

Parent: "I recognize that Hattie Sue has trouble getting along with others. But she does not want to come to any group program. She says that other kids would pick on her and get her into trouble. We don't like pushing her into things she doesn't want to do."

Practitioner: "There are a few issues to keep in mind when you are trying to decide how to deal with Hattie Sue. We need to appreciate that coming to the social competence group is recognition that something is wrong and that this can be scary to some children. In my experience her angry behaviors don't seem to get better with time. In fact, the longer they go on, the harder it may be to change them. With continued social isolation we are running the risk that Hattie Sue will become depressed."

A number of strategies can be used to facilitate active participation of the child in the process of goal setting. As a result of the assessment, the social problems of the child typically emerge. The practitioner can reframe the issues into meaningful statements that the child can understand. For example, the adult could say, "You seem to be telling me that you would like to be better at . . ." skills such as playing with others during recess, learning to manage a bully, or winning and losing; through continued discussion, goals are developed and confirmed by the child. Another strategy is for the practitioner to provide choices of goals, either verbally or through a written list, and allow the child to choose two or three. This method is particularly applicable to younger children. A final approach is to have the child complete a questionnaire such as the Self-Awareness Assessment described in Chapter 8. The completed form then serves as a stimulus for discussion of preferred goals.

Goals for Individual Children

When running a social competence program, the practitioner typically creates individual and group goals to guide intervention. The goals should be based on each aspect of the conceptual framework in order to assure comprehensive coverage of the child's social needs. A wide variety of individual goals are listed in each of the following categories of the framework. Although there are different methods to writing goals and objectives, the subsequent examples illustrate one format in which the child's name introduces the goal or objective statement, as in "Billy will participate with his classmates on the playground jungle gym for at least 5 minutes at morning recess." Practitioners will probably need to modify this style in order to meet the mandates of different work settings; IEP requirements, for example, may necessitate a more focused behavioral objective format than a private practice requires. Note that the samples can apply to different contexts such as the school, home, and community.

Purpose of Interaction

Instrumental Interactions

- Borrow art supplies during cooperative projects.
- Plan weekend sleepovers with a good friend.
- Request swapping toys during play.
- Organize a baseball card collection with a friend.

Social-Emotional Interactions

- Develop a close friendship.
- Make small talk with classmates when waiting in line.

- Arrange to eat with at least two peers at lunch.
- Discuss and empathize with a friend about shared disappointments.

World View

Social Perspective Taking

- Acknowledge the ideas of peers at least twice during sessions of the social competence group.
- Notice the response of peers to his or her actions.
- Recognize when someone can use assistance and offer it.
- Decrease discounting and "me first" behaviors.

Components of Social Competence

Social and Play Behavior

- Develop age appropriate friendships at school.
- Play cooperatively with two peers during recess.
- Decrease whining and tantrum throwing when not getting his or her way in social situations.
- Demonstrate playful bantering when hanging out with peers.

Prosocial Skills

- Expand turn taking by playing with his brother once a day at home with a favorite toy.
- Increase interpersonal behaviors by going to the park and playing with two unfamiliar children on the jungle gym.
- Initiate membership in a community group of his or her choice, such as Girl Scouts or a soccer team.
- Demonstrate the ability to give and accept feedback.

Self-Regulation

- Position the chair a comfortable distance from another classmate during lunch time.
- Decrease the tendency to interrupt peers during conversation.
- Modulate one's emotional state and activity level to match the demands of the situation.
- Decrease attention-seeking behaviors during social studies class.

Communication

- Share relevant experiences and ideas without repetition after one verbal prompt from an adult.
- Increase the ability to maintain relevant topics and ask appropriate questions when conversing with peers.
- Decrease "exaggerations" and fabrications during conversation.
- Expand social perception by noticing when the listener has heard enough.

Social Decision Making

- Improve problem identification by recognizing when a peer is angry and stating the peer's feelings.

- Consider possible consequences of a choice instead of jumping to a conclusion.

- Increase repertoire of strategies for solving conflicts.

- Improve the implementation of problem-solving strategies with coaching by an adult.

Table 9.1 provides sample individual goals to address specific needs of children according to the common behavioral profiles discussed in Chapter 7. The goals are representative of the presenting needs of these different types if children.

Table 9.1
Sample Goals of Common Behavioral Profiles

Behavioral Profile	Sample Goals
Egocentric	Limit bossiness by decreasing "me first" behaviors.
	Increase social flexibility through active listening to the ideas of peers.
	Accept the viewpoint of others on occasion.
	Get along with sister during short car trips.
Language Difficulty	Increase the use of language to regulate his emotional state.
	Engage in reciprocal one-to-one conversations.
	Expand the ability to pose and respond to questions.
	Notice the nonverbal response of the listener before acting.
Controlling	Decrease the tendency to make social interactions competitive.
	Increase persistence in activities that he finds challenging or did not choose.
	Expand negotiating skills by accepting the suggestions of peers when planning joint activities.
	Decrease manipulating behavior with other children during recess.
Scared	Increase appropriate assertiveness during play with peers.
	Expand risk taking by trying out new experiences.
	Recognize when he needs help and spontaneously asks for it.
Limit Testing	Responds promptly and positively to requests by adults.
	Reduce the tendency to bend and alter the rules when playing games.
	Allow others to participate in conversations without monopolizing the topic.
	Decrease angry outbursts when others are in charge.

Group Goals for Intervention

In addition to individual goals, shared goals for the social competence group as a whole are useful, as group goals provide a focus and cohesion for intervention planning. Typically, a group has no more than two or three common goals.

In creating group goals, the practitioner first looks at the individual goals of all participants in order to identify common themes. Should a number of the children have a shared problem, that issue would be a natural candidate for a group goal. Sometimes the individual goals constitute the components of a larger group goal; for example, there may be a cluster of individual goals around self-regulation and social decision-making that can be integrated into a shared group goal such as, "The group will successfully plan and carry-out play activities with all members participating." In addition, one child may have a glaring problem that warrants attention as a group goal; for instance, a child having problems with self-regulation may be so physically intrusive that most social exchanges are impeded. In order to benefit from the group experience, this difficulty needs to be attended to first. Otherwise it is a barrier to the child's participation and the effective dynamics of the group. Such a goal would also be developmentally beneficial to all group members and could be written as, "Group members will respect the personal space of each other."

Group goals must also be developmentally sensible, meaning that the goals are matched to the emerging abilities of the children. Goals that are too advanced and unattainable are deceptively easy to set. For example, the practitioner may write group goals that address cooperative play when in reality the children do not have the prerequisite skills for this level of play, or a global goal such as "improve self-esteem" may be too complex and abstract a construct. Rather, the group would benefit from focusing on a goal of increasing competence in a particular behavior or social skill that could then indirectly influence self-esteem; the goal could be, "Group members will exchange praise for jobs well done at the conclusion of an activity."

When developing goals, the practitioner must remember that initially, all children in a social competence group automatically share at least two goals. First, the children need to establish a comfort level in the setting and attachment to the group. Second, they need to learn the rules and expectations of the group setting. These goals pertain to the initial sessions in which the children are first participating in the group.

Goals, whether individual or group, need to be continuously reevaluated as to their relevance and altered as necessary. Due to the complexity of children, revisions are sometimes required after repeated sessions of getting to know the children better. Indeed, some problem behaviors may not be evident until a number of weeks into the program.

Intervention

Group Program Overview

There are many ways to design a group program to foster social development that is based on the conceptual framework. This chapter describes a standard format that we have used for more than 15 years with some supportive efficacy data in Chapter 14. The practitioner is encouraged to adapt this design to the uniqueness of each setting.

This chapter discusses issues in determining the membership in a group (such as group size, age, gender, and behavioral composition) and describes the four segments of a typical group format: conversation time, short-term activity, project activity, and closure. Common behavioral problems typically experienced during each segment are discussed.

The typical group that we lead has 8–10 children; these children have difficulties in the social arena but may not have a medical diagnosis or educational classification. The most common special needs in many of our groups include attention deficit disorder with or without hyperactivity, language impairments, and learning disabilities. Two adults serve as facilitators so that the needs of each child can be addressed in addition to the focus on group process. The practitioners can represent the same or different disciplines; a very rich combination is to have an occupational therapist with a speech pathologist, special educator, or a psychosocial clinician such as a social worker or psychologist.

In this model, the groups meet on a weekly basis for 1 to 2 hours. An intervention cycle is composed of 12 weeks, and as the groups are run on a fall, spring, and summer cycle, children are able to maintain participation over time if it is indicated. Children usually make their best developmental gains at the beginning and the end of their involvement in a group. Therefore, if possible children should participate in a series of short-term experiences rather than signing up for one long, open-ended experience. The cycle format also provides an opportunity to reevaluate the child's program, make needed changes, and graduate the child to a more advanced group if indicated.

Group Membership

A number of considerations exist regarding group composition. The potential success of a group often rests on decisions made in the very beginning of the planning process; for instance, a group of inappropriate size and composition can undermine the therapeutic value of the program. There are occasions when groups are predetermined and essentially inherited by the practitioner; for example, a teacher may work with an entire class or a therapist may be assigned a group of children by a child study team. However, the following guidelines are useful when the practitioner can influence the unique composition of a group.

Group Size

In our model we prefer 8 to 10 children with two adults. This ratio allows for truly therapeutic, personalized intervention. A group of fewer than five children may have difficulty maintaining adequate attendance and a viable group size. On occasion, due to the severity of the children's problems or their young ages, a small group of three children may be formed to work on basic developmental skills. At the most, a group should have 13 to 14 children, provided there is ample space and three adults. A lead practitioner needs to be responsible for the overall flow of the group process. Of course, our group model can be adapted for larger groups such as school classes and scouts. In the case of larger groups, the children can be divided into smaller units for specific activities; if this is not possible and the group must be managed as a whole, the adult modifies the goals, outcomes, and activities of the group to accommodate this group size.

Age

We often run separate groups for the following age ranges: ages 3–5, ages 5–7, ages 7–9, and ages 10–12. In general, a 2- to 3-year spread is workable. In reality the children often have individual profiles of strengths and weaknesses that add complexity to the group. For instance, a very bright but socially immature child may work well with older children, or a parent may be concerned that a child only plays with younger children. The practitioner must assess if same age peers are best for the child or whether a different age group would be more therapeutic. The child's chronological age is not the only determinant for group assignment; the parents and practitioners must collaborate to determine the optimal placement.

Gender

Boys and girls mix easily in a group when they are between ages 3 and 9 or 10, as during this period the children are typically accepting of differences. However, in some groups there may be a clustering of boys with boys and girls with girls during some activities. In early adolescence the children may prefer same age peers, chum groups, and exhibit strong activity preferences; consequently, the focus of the group tends to shift as children approach this age, with the creation of a carpentry group for boys, a personal appearance group for girls, etc. This is a time when same sex youth enjoy hanging out together.

A reality in programming is that boys are referred more frequently with social skills difficulties. Boys tend to be more visible because of externalizing behaviors such as physical overactivity, boisterous behavior, and acting out; likewise, boys are more obvious than girls when they are shy and withdrawn. Often a social competence group will have a majority of male members. If the girls are also socially immature with inadequate prosocial skills and perspective taking, the mixed group composition is not critical. Parents are usually concerned if their child is the only girl in a group, as they prefer at least one other girl for social bonding and girl talk, and under these circumstances the practitioner may choose to delay placing the child in a group until another girl is available.

Behavioral Composition

Every child has a unique profile of strengths and weaknesses related to his or her social competence. In constructing a group, the practitioner wants heterogeneity but enough similarities among the children so that they can bond. It would be highly inadvisable to have a group solely consist of shy children or children with excessively high energy. A medical diagnosis such as oppositional defiant disorder or attention deficit hyperactivity disorder does not preclude a child from placement in a group. However, the group focus must stay on social development and not on behavior management. If the child's behavior is too extreme, the child needs to receive individual intervention until adequate self-regulation is established.

A last consideration is that one wants more than one child with a particular strength or vulnerability in the group; for instance, one would not want only one child with a major communication problem in a highly verbal group, as this child would not fit in without a similar peer. Likewise, a child who has good ideas and takes charge needs to be balanced by another child who is equally strong, because while together neither of the children is likely to become bossy and controlling. As the practitioner determines the composition of the group, he or she considers different ways to pair and combine the children according to their behavioral profiles; the children are clustered differently based on the activities and therapeutic goals.

Session Segments

An intervention session has a typical structure of four segments.

1. A conversation time helps the group to coalesce.

2. The short-term activity is usually a gross motor experience to facilitate social interaction and to discharge energy.

3. The project activity enhances many facets of social competence over multiple sessions.

4. Closure is usually a snack within a social context, accompanied by a review of the session.

This standard format provides a balanced program but can be modified in different ways for different children. The following discussion describes each segment, identifies its therapeutic goals, provides guidelines for conducting the segment, and presents strategies to address targeted behaviors.

Conversation Time

The intervention session begins with conversation time, during which the children discuss what happened in the preceding week, and the plan for the current session is previewed. This segment lasts 15 to 20 minutes. Conversation time focuses on communication, addresses social-emotional issues, and is critical for establishing the emotional tone for the group, a sense of group cohesion, and attachment to the group. For some groups, this segment may be called circle time, news time, or personal sharing.

There are five primary group goals for conversation time.

1. To enhance listening, attending, and remembering to improve the individual's focus on what other group members are sharing.

2. To shift from monologue to dialogue as egocentricity decreases and communication skills improve.

3. To practice language skills with an emphasis on discourse and pragmatics.

4. To teach and practice prosocial skills such as greeting, introducing self and others, and complimenting.

5. To shift from instrumental to social-emotional interactions where group members practice sharing personal and affective information.

Conversation time is a very powerful component of the session because every child has "center stage" visibility in an accepting environment. This personal reinforcement enhances group attachment because the children feel as if they belong.

Within each group, the purpose and format for conversation time must be explained; expectations for the segment should be discussed and rules for conduct established. Each group will have a somewhat different set of rules related to the developmental level of the children and these must be stated in understandable language. For instance, rules for a preschool group may include *use your indoor voice, wait your turn,* and *ask before you touch.* The rules for an older group may focus on two primary issues, those of not hurting anyone's feelings and not harming anyone physically. The children must know that they are safe in the group and that they will be protected from verbal or physical abuse. Many children have long histories of failure and humiliation in group settings, so a climate of trust and safety is essential for any engagement and attachment to the group.

Conversation time is an excellent opportunity for the children to orient themselves to each other and to develop group cohesion. The children first share personal information with the group; for example, they can take turns saying three things about themselves. For a new or young group, adults can introduce topics for conversation to provide structure; common topics include favorite food, color, sport or TV show, school trips, vacations, pets, special events such as birthdays, and family composition such as siblings.

There are a number of follow-up activities that can be conducted during conversation time or the short-term segment to help the children solidify what they have learned about each other.

1. Passing games (listed under Ball Play in Chapter 13) have the children identify different characteristics of each other as they roll a ball back and forth in the circle.

2. In the "Mystery Person" game children write descriptions of themselves and place these in a bag. Each child pulls out a description and guesses to whom it belongs (described under Who Am I? in Chapter 13).

3. In "The Roving Reporter" activity one child interviews another about his or her name, interests, or special experiences and introduces that individual to the group in the style of a reporter (see Interviewing in Chapter 13).

Activities that teach the components of a conversation are conducted in the whole group during the conversation segment. The adults demonstrate and facilitate such skills as introducing a topic, choosing a topic of interest to group members, shifting from a monologue to a dialogue, and responding to the comments of others. Interviewing activities are excellent for practicing conversational skills. Without these skills children remain egocentric and may talk only about themselves, may misunderstand when peers make comments or ask questions, and may not participate in the topics of others. These egocentric children need the more formal instruction and practice provided in the total group setting. When they start to spontaneously interact with each other, the practitioner knows that the children are ready for conversation time in smaller groups. The practitioner should not expect intimate conversation to occur in a large group format.

With older children, conversation can be a very informal time during which the children hang out and play tabletop pinball, cards, or other games. This version of conversation time could be misinterpreted and viewed as if nothing were happening, but in reality, the social engagement of older children tends to be very casual, trendy, blasé, and indifferent. For children who are socially immature, the adults may actually coach them to act like their age peers. When adolescent girls hang out they establish a sense of self by labeling traits of their peers. Within their cliques they focus on gossiping about everyone and creating hierarchies of desirability centered on popularity, physical attractiveness, talents, and skills. They use vocabulary that is fashionable slang and, therefore, frequently changing. A girl who has language problems may not be able to compete in this social circuit if her speed of processing is too slow, word retrieval is problematic, or conversation is taken too literally and not understood for its abstract meaning. These everyday problems are demonstrated and addressed during conversation time.

Over years of experience conducting social competence groups, we have observed a number of maladaptive social behaviors that tend to occur during conversation time; behaviors that represent the problems that the children have in their social relationships. The practitioner needs to be prepared to manage them. The following list highlights some of the most common problems displayed during this segment of the group. The introduction of these behaviors offers a chance to deal with them therapeutically; if problem behaviors are never spontaneously demonstrated during the group, the practitioner has little opportunity to address them in a naturalistic context.

Butting In

Some children have a habit of interrupting the conversation of others; these children may be egocentric and unable to take turns. For these children an object such as a baton can be used to identify who is allowed to talk as it is passed to the designated speaker. While the speaker holds the object, no one else can speak until the baton is passed on to the next child who wants to respond. Often this structure markedly diminishes "butting in" during conversation time. Another reason that children may demonstrate this behavior is because of attentional problems, which can cause them to have difficulty waiting without losing their thoughts. A notebook can be given to these children so that they can jot down their thoughts for reference when it is their time to speak.

Discounting

A major cause of rejection by peers is the tendency to discount the statements of others as the child negates the speaker's statements by unnecessarily correcting them. For instance, Davey remarked, "I went to the beach and found cool shells." Ethan responded, "But the Jersey shore has lousy shells since they restored the beaches." Later in the conversation Davey commented, "I'm really excited by my word processing program because it will help me with my school work." Ethan responded, "Yeah, but the new Windows program allows you to do everything." As a result of these exchanges, Davey decided to avoid Ethan, who made him feel "stupid." Children like Ethan may demonstrate discounting as a result of their egocentricity; they are driven by facts, a need to be right, and an inability to consider the perspective of others.

Other children, however, are mean-spirited in their discounting and put down other children in a "one-upmanship" fashion. For example, Trudie mentioned, "I am collecting cards of the World Series Yankees team," and Rashid countered, "I already have the whole set!" This comment was delivered to make Trudie feel diminished and Rashid appear superior.

An effective way to decrease discounting is to engage the discounter in a dialogue privately, out of the hearing of others, because this is an instructional opportunity rather than a punishment. This dialogue needs to cover three components. The practitioner and child should develop a cueing system so that the child recognizes when he or she uses the discounting behavior. Also, the practitioner should help the discounter consider the impact of his or her behavior on others, and how it can make others feel diminished, sad, or angry. And, the private dialogue can help the discounter realize the opinion that other children have of him or her as a result of this behavior. This three-fold strategy only works if the child has a desire to be liked by the other children.

Silliness

Some children demonstrate an excessive amount of silliness and giddiness or to provoke such behavior in others during conversation time; the key to managing this behavior is to identify the presenting cause. If used to get attention, silliness in behavior is best ignored; praising the actions of others in the group while ignoring the child who is acting silly can be a potent motivator for the child to change his or her behavior.

If the child is acting silly because of overarousal and excitability, the practitioner needs to help the child to calm down. A high emotional state may be due to the child's excitement in entering the group; many children become aroused when transitioning between activities. During conversation time the adult can employ the practitioner's conscious use of self to assist the child to self-regulate by sitting next to the child, putting a soothing hand on the child's arm, using a slow soft voice, previewing the schedule for the session, and decreasing the pace of the group.

Sometimes children are silly due to anxiety. Conversation time can be especially anxiety-ridden for children with language difficulties, and simplifying a task so that the children are not overwhelmed can reduce tension. For example, group members can be told to make only one comment or pose only one question. By adding a concrete reinforcement such as tokens for holding appropriate conversation, the group members are motivated to stop acting silly.

Boring Monologue

Some children do not demonstrate reciprocal interaction in their conversational style and tend to dominate the conversation with a boring monologue. This pattern, which is highly detrimental to the development of friendships, is often seen during conversation time. There are at least four possible components to this problem.

1. Some children have a nonverbal language disorder in which they do not comprehend when the listener has heard enough. Other children are visually inattentive and do not notice signs of tedium such as gaze aversion, slouching of the body, or fidgeting. In both circumstances, the practitioner encourages the children to scan everyone in the group and look for any signs of waning interest.

2. Some children have difficulty organizing their ideas and presenting them in a concise manner; as a result, the conversation of some of these children is tangential. During conversation time the practitioner can have the children choose two sentences that tell the most important ideas about what they want to say; group members ask them relevant questions, and they are coached to limit their answers to the specific question. Elaboration is not allowed because the children are to practice being responsive to the conversational partner. When needed, the adults can role-play this interaction.

3. Some children use a dull, pedantic, monotonous voice that presents information in an alienating and uninteresting manner. Intervention focuses on the adult modeling a playful, dramatic, and childlike affect. Some direct teaching may be required so that the children learn to understand that messages are related to their tone of voice. For instance, the child is asked to identify the feelings of an experience and the practitioner points out any discrepancy in vocal quality, such as describing a fun trip to an amusement park in a monotonous voice.

4. Some children conduct monologues because they do not understand the reciprocity inherent in a conversation. They deliver their discourse as if it were a report and become furious if interrupted. These children often respond well to direct instruction and coaching.

Bullying and Teasing

Bullying and teasing behaviors are never tolerated in the group, as each constitutes a major violation of the group rule that words and actions cannot be used to hurt others. When bullying or teasing occurs, a number of intervention strategies can be implemented. The practitioner reiterates the cardinal rule that harmful words and actions are unacceptable; this declaration provides support and protection to the victim and peers, and psychological and physical safety is assured for all.

Then, the bully is taken aside and his or her behavior is discussed; the child should not be spoken to publicly. At first, the conversation attempts to determine the child's awareness of the behavior and its impact, as well as the motivation for the behavior. The adult's attitude should be one of a concerned fact-finder and should not have a judgmental perspective. The consequences of the bullying behavior are made explicit to the child; for instance, the child may not be able to participate in some of the highly motivating and enjoyable activities. Such exclusion can be a strong enticement to alter behavior. For the bully who is basically insecure, the practitioner provides opportunities for the child to be a leader and to shine. Often this positive recognition and reinforcement reduces the need for the bullying behavior.

Sometimes during conversation time a child will share an experience about being bullied, and the group can problem-solve together ways for the child to handle similar situations in the future. First, ideas are generated about what the victim could do. Next, some of the children can role-play a bullying incident and its management while the targeted child observes and learns. Then, the targeted child practices the behavior and role-plays with others. The experience of being picked on and teased is common among these children and often fosters an emotionally charged discussion.

Inattention

Inattention during conversation time may be related to a number of factors. Some children may be distracted by internal stimuli such as fatigue, hyperarousal, or the need to go to the bathroom. Distractibility for others may be due to the inability to screen out the sounds and sights of the group setting. Other children are inattentive because they are thinking about what will happen next and therefore do not listen. Modifying the activity schedule can increase or decrease arousal based on the desired effect. For example, a physical activity can increase attention, or a snack can refuel and refresh the children, while younger children can be reminded to go to the bathroom before the group session begins.

Decreasing the complexity and distractibility of the environment can help focus the children. An effective way to calm and orient inattentive children is for the practitioner to suddenly become silent; once all eyes are on the adult, the activity can resume. Another modification is the posting of an easily visible schedule that allows forward-thinking children to preview and review the agenda. Also, if a child is taking medication for an attentional disorder, all relevant parties should discuss whether the child's medication schedule covers the group session.

With maturation of the group there is a decrease in the occurrence of the maladaptive social behaviors. As they become more skillful, the children engage spontaneously in social conversation during this segment of the group, becoming eager to participate in conversation time and developing an attachment to their peers. The role of the practitioner changes during this evolution. From a leadership role as teacher and coach, the adult becomes a facilitator as needed.

Short-Term Activity

The next segment of a typical social competence group is a short-term activity lasting 15 to 20 minutes. Often a gross motor activity is used to help the children discharge energy in a social context, helping the children become organized and ready for the subsequent activities. The gross motor experience is particularly important if the group is conducted at the end of the day or after a time period when the children were sedentary. The primary goals of the short-term activity are to promote self-regulation, social and play behavior, and prosocial skills. Activity selection can be specifically tailored to expand the play repertoire of individual children in the group. One activity is commonly chosen for the segment, with variations explored; sample gross motor activities include obstacle courses, relays, balloon volleyball, hot potato, ball play, and "Duck, Duck, Goose." The practitioner may choose an activity that is not gross motor in nature; effective choices for such activities include floor puzzles, mime phrases, "Where's Waldo?" and "Who am I?" Most of these activities can be designed for the whole group, teams, partners, or individual participation.

Certain maladaptive social behaviors are characteristically demonstrated during the short-term activity. Particularly if gross motor intervention is used, there is a tendency to elicit aggressiveness, excessive competition, inflexible thinking, poor teamwork, and motor incoordination. The practitioner needs to anticipate the emergence of these behaviors and be prepared to manage them. Children with learning disabilities often demonstrate these behaviors in their academic work; in this case the behaviors occur in a play situation.

Aggressiveness

During short-term activities the children may demonstrate poor self-regulation by being too active and loud, using excessive force such as body slamming, and yelling out expressions of anger. Children need to have a physical release of their aggressive tension. They can be encouraged to channel their aggressiveness through vigorous creative games or physical activities. Excellent gross motor activities include ball play, relays, parachute, cooperative musical chairs, and start/stop activities such as "Red Light, Green Light" and "Statues." Emotional release through laughter and squealing is also beneficial for dissipating extreme aggressiveness. By decreasing the arousal state and shifting the emotional tone, the children are more open to receiving feedback about how to control their behavior. Behavior management techniques are implemented in combination with these strategies. For example, the adult establishes behavioral contracts with the children that define expectations to be met within the short-term activity.

Excessive Competition

Children with excessive competition have a total focus on winning even if the game is not inherently competitive. Where no challenge exists, they will create one, like competing to see who can get his or her shoes on the fastest, or racing to be first through a door. They obsess in an egocentric manner about "coming in first" and quickly lose sight of teamwork in collaborative activities. These children may have good prosocial skills if they can monitor their competitiveness.

Three methods are successful for dealing with children who exhibit extreme competition.

1. Coaching can provide immediate feedback to their behaviors. Coaching must be gentle so the children do not feel humiliated or reprimanded; therefore, their arousal stays at a manageable level enabling them to apply the suggestions to their behavior.

2. Observation and modeling are also effective methods. These children usually enjoy physical, sports-like activities and are highly motivated to return to an activity after being temporarily removed. They may be asked to observe other children in the group who are exemplars of desired cooperative behavior and be "a detective" so they can report back what the others are doing. The adult validates the points being made regarding the correct way to play the game and gives these children another chance to participate.

3. Another method for enhancing collaborative behavior is to highlight leadership. Because many have leadership potential, these children are placed in a leadership role in the group with clear definitions regarding how to act in that capacity. The children experience how to facilitate teamwork in others; for instance, they learn how to focus on cooperation instead of individualism. This leadership role channels their competitiveness into affirmative, prosocial behaviors.

Inflexible thinking

Children who are inflexible in their thinking have problems in learning, interpreting, and following rules. They may think concretely and be unable to set aside the rules for the larger goal of having fun; this pattern is similar to "discounting" children who are driven by facts to the detriment of social engagement. Other children have problems in managing multiple attentional demands, trying to juggle cognitive information and sensorimotor input simultaneously. These children often fix on a part of the activity and ignore the rest. Still other children have a temperamental need to be in control and are thus rigid in their behavior.

Practitioners can increase the level of playfulness in these children by shifting the focus from playing by the rules to having fun. The rules of an activity can be frequently changed to add a dimension of novelty and enjoyment; for instance, the activity can be altered on a weekly basis. Another strategy is to give the children the opportunity to make the rules. For tasks that have multiple attentional demands, the various steps are introduced and practiced by the children before they are expected to put them together, and when the children attempt the integrated, complex task, they are already familiar with the component parts. Some children decide what the rules mean in a narrow fashion and rigidly follow their interpretation. Reviewing the rules of a game on a regular basis and posting these rules as a written list assist the children in accepting the group's consensus about the rules.

Motor Incoordination

During the period of the short-term activity, children may exhibit gross and fine motor difficulties and appear slow, "klutzy," or disorganized. These children may resist participation because they are aware of their problems. The practitioner needs to differentiate between the child who has poor attention and self-regulation and the child who has motor incoordination. Both sets of children can look the same but require different intervention.

Children are embarrassed by being conspicuously unsuccessful during activities. An immediate therapeutic goal is to protect these children from emotional harm; if they feel emotionally safe, most children will attempt the activities that are presented. If, however, a child still does not want to participate, this wish should be honored. There are many ways to maintain a connection with the activity such as recording team results, retrieving the ball, or monitoring the stopwatch. Another option is to decrease the complexity of the motor tasks so that they are graded to the skill level of all the children in the group. Opportunities may also be provided for clumsy children to use other skills within the task; for example, a child may not do so well in a relay but shine when the retrieved puzzle pieces are assembled.

Project Activity

The project activity is the heart of the social competence group for four primary reasons. This activity addresses all aspects of the conceptual framework and gives ample time for the children to practice the component skills. As in the previous segments, activity analysis is creatively applied to address individual and group goals. The project activity promotes evolution of the group process over time, and the children have the opportunity to play using spontaneous social behaviors. The project activity most clearly distinguishes our intervention approach from an instructional approach for developing social skills.

This is the longest segment of the group session and lasts approximately 30 minutes. The project activity occurs over multiple sessions, either as one long-term complex project or a series of small but related projects. An example of a long-term complex project is the creation of a jungle scene by a group of young children during five sessions. The group called themselves "The Lions" because that animal is king of the jungle. Based on this theme, the children built a life-size jungle setting including palm trees, banana trees, a lion's den, snakes, and other jungle animals. Upon completion of the jungle, they spent the following several weeks playing imaginatively within it. Other long-term projects are: creating collages, preparing for celebrations or a magic show, constructing a zoo or town, writing and videotaping a play, and making life-size portraits.

An example of series of small, related projects is to have the children make constructions over a number of weeks. A sequence could begin with small groups or pairs who are assigned materials and structures to build. Over the following weeks they are rotated through the various materials and building assignments, and eventually they are allowed to choose materials, plan what to build, and pick play partners. Another illustration of small, related projects is to learn old-fashioned games. The children interview their parents about what favorite indoor games they had when they were children, and then learn those games, which may include pick-up sticks, marbles, and card games. During group sessions, the children teach these games to their peer group, and once all games are learned, free play sessions occur.

During the project activity segment, difficulties can arise related to all components of the conceptual framework. Problems in self-regulation are typically seen in poor frustration tolerance and perseverance within the activities. The children often have deficits in social decision-making related to determining a common goal, developing a plan of action, and problem solving. Communication can be an area of weakness due to the inability to share ideas, follow directions, and read nonverbal cues. This issue may also be related to egocentricity, in which the children fail to take the viewpoint of others. The project activity provides a rich opportunity to address these common behaviors within a controlled play context.

There are additional points to keep in mind when planning and implementing the project activity. This segment of the intervention session may emphasize teaching specific developmental skills that are not in the children's play repertoire; a number of sessions can be dedicated to helping the children learn an age-appropriate activity such as playing four square or making model airplanes. The initial focus on skill acquisition prepares the children for use of the skills in a social context. The practitioner may choose to teach the most current fad so that the children have a common reference point with their peers.

The practitioner makes conscious decisions about how to cluster the children for the project activity. In general, children are asked to function in pairs before expanding the number of peer participants. Social decision making, which is very complex developmentally, can be particularly enhanced on a one-to-one basis between partners. In addition, the practitioner may choose to keep the same pairs of children together over time in order to foster intimacy and attachment. Rotating the children within pairs is more demanding because the children have to adjust to the personality and style of each partner; however the rotation fosters relationships with all group members, and therefore, group cohesion.

The role of the practitioner is dynamic and shifts according to the needs of the group. At times, the adult models and role-plays desired behaviors and offers direct teaching. At other times the adult decreases his or her level of involvement and intervenes only on occasion as a coach or a resource; occasionally the adult may join the children in play as another participant. Within any activity or group session the adult may need to assume any of these multiple roles based on the changing requirements of the children. This is a complex example of the practitioner's conscious use of self.

It is important to keep a focus on goals related to social competence and not to become sidetracked with skill training or activity completion. Skills are the building blocks for growth, whereas social competence is the integration and application of those skills in a social context. Therapeutic work directed toward teaching skills must be simultaneously linked to its social objective. Otherwise the social outcome may be forgotten and the group work merely reinforces isolated developmental skills of the children. Likewise, it is easy to be seduced by the project so that everyone focuses solely on the quality of the end product. The interactive process of participating in the activity is most important, and not the finished product.

Many children who have problems in social skills have a long history of failure and isolation; they are exceptionally sensitive to social slights and can be considered emotionally fragile. Even children with externalizing problem behaviors such as aggression, bossiness, and discounting are often concealing hidden pain. During any intervention session the children are challenged to confront some of their weaknesses and limitations. They require sensitive emotional support to sustain engagement and decrease the likelihood of resistance. The adult needs to assure that every group member has an opportunity to succeed and shine.

Closure

The last segment of the group, closure, is an opportunity to summarize the highlights of the session. This segment can be called closing time, wrap up, or a similar description. The goals of the session can be revisited with a discussion of how group members performed, and outside assignments may be given so that the children will practice skills in the following week. Closure is also a time to preview activities for the next session and typically involves 15 minutes of conversation; some groups conduct closure during snack time. Closure is the time to preview and review, receive peer feedback, and transition from the group. Another important function of closure is for the children to adjust their activity level to the next setting, as the children should not leave the group too stimulated and excitable. Leave-taking is an essential prosocial skill that is practiced during closure.

If the practitioner decides to let the group have a snack during closing time, it creates an intimate, playful, and fun environment. The children practice casual conversation as they enjoy their preferred foods, and eating is an opportunity to work on many social skills. Prosocial niceties associated with meals are taught and practiced, including saying "please" and "thank you," as well as eating with a closed mouth. Frequently, one child is designated as the host and assigned to bring in the snack. The host is expected to show appropriate etiquette for serving the food and promoting small talk, while the other group members must demonstrate the behavior of a proper guest. The social responsibilities of all the children are emphasized, such as cleaning up after their snack. There may be occasions when social decision-making is required; for example, the children may have to decide how to distribute the remaining two cupcakes when there are four children who want seconds. Motor problems are frequently observed during snack time, such as the clumsy child who spills the juice and is covered with crumbs. The child who has to exert major effort in motor control will be less able to attend to social manners at the same time.

There are many transitions that occur throughout the group experience, including entering the group, moving from one activity to another, and eventually leaving. Transitions are commonly hard for some children who need strong structure and guidelines, as the children are apprehensive about what is to happen next. Others find it hard to let go of what they are doing and moving on to the next task; they may be rigid and inflexible or simply enjoying the current activity. For other children with problems in self-regulation, waiting during the transition is demanding, as they are impatient during the time of change.

The following suggestions may be helpful for planning and managing transitions. The first consideration is to allow adequate time for transitions to occur and not hurry children unrealistically between tasks. Analyzing transition time facilitates breaking down the task into component steps that can be previewed with the children to prepare them for transition. Likewise, reviewing a transition that has just occurred will foster a sense of continuity. Children who have trouble waiting can be given a job to fill the time, such as putting chairs away. A transition place can be designated for children to go during down time; this "waiting spot" provides structure and focus.

Group Dynamics

In this chapter, group dynamics are addressed because they are therapeutically designed to foster peer interaction and the group process. In addition, intervention techniques are reviewed that enhance social competence.

Group dynamics emphasize the forces that influence relationships among members and eventually the group outcome. Practitioners actively monitor and foster both group process and group development. Group process involves the interpersonal relationships of the participants and reflects what is happening in the moment between and among members. Group development refers to a series of predictable stages that groups progress through over time. The practitioner is deliberately influencing the group process of the individual session and the development of the group over a series of weeks and months.

Group process has been addressed throughout the discussion on assessment and intervention and was reflected in the narrative related to the four segments of an intervention session. In some ways all of the intervention recommendations, activities, and case examples incorporate the elements of group process; indeed, our intervention frame of reference uses group process as a major vehicle for effecting change in children.

Group Development

Social competence groups evolve through essentially four stages, which are similar to those described by Cole (1993). The first stage of group development is orientation, during which the group is actively establishing a structure and focus for itself and members are developing a dependency on the group leader. In the second stage (conflict) difficulties with the leader arise and there is a period of testing and stress. In the third stage (trust and cohesion) group members experience positive interpersonal relationships and a sense of intimacy and attachment; during this time there is a commitment to the goals and activities of the group. In the last stage, or termination, the children are able to separate from the group with a sense that it was a positive experience.

Not all groups or individuals progress through these stages. For instance, a group's membership can be so diverse that the group never gels and therefore does not evolve developmentally. Likewise, an individual child may have a characteristic that unexpectedly slows his or her rate of change compared to the group as a whole. In both of these cases, the developmental progression is arrested. In general, the practitioner wants to move the children through all these stages.

Orientation

In this initial stage of group development the members are getting to know each other and the rules of the group. Personal relationships are beginning to be made with the practitioner; there is a tendency for the children to focus on the adult and to ignore their peers, and the adult must redirect their attention to each other. The children are concerned during this stage with whether they fit in, are respected, and are safe to be themselves. The newness of the group tends to foster attention seeking, narcissism, overtalking, and possessiveness. Although indicative of the orientation stage, these behaviors may persist in some children as major presenting behaviors. Because some children have a history of failure in groups, this period should be fun and safe. In a weekly group the orientation stage may last 2 to 3 weeks. Even if the children are familiar with each other, it is essential to have an orientation phase to help cement relationships.

There are numerous activities that facilitate the orientation stage, including ball play, statues, and board games with partners. We have found the following activities particularly effective.

- **Mystery person** — Children write descriptions of themselves and place them in a bag. Each child pulls out a description and guesses to whom it belongs.

- **Roving reporter** — One child interviews another about his or her name, favorite activities, and interests. The child then serves as a reporter and introduces that individual to the group (see Interviewing in the verbal section of Chapter 13).

- **Find your fellow animal** — Children are asked to pretend to be specific animals. At least two of the children have the same animal. The children act out the animals and try to find a peer who is the same animal.

Conflict

During this stage, there is a natural expression of challenge and rebellion over issues related to power and authority, accompanied by a tendency to be slightly mistrustful and ambivalent about the practitioner. The children disagree about the rules of the group, its structure, and who should be in charge. This normal stage of conflict is influenced by a number of factors. For some children the issues are power and control; for other children resistance emerges because they are confronting their social limitations by participating in the group. Yet other children are well-mannered during the orientation stage but demonstrate their social problems once they feel somewhat comfortable. There are also children during the conflict stage who stay a bit disengaged, aloof, or passive due to lack of commitment to the group.

The adult must recognize that the conflict stage is a normal phase of group development. The practitioner should not overreact and take the group behaviors as a personal affront but rather as a time-limited phenomenon as long as the leadership struggle is managed properly. While the children are testing the limits, the adult needs to avoid the two extremes of becoming overly authoritarian or giving up control of the group. The best option is to demonstrate a collaborative style in which there is some flexibility in setting rules and clear boundaries for acceptable behavior. Disagreements are inevitable and acceptable; the issue is for the children to learn to move from bossiness and rigidity to prosocial persuasiveness. Thus this stage is a major opportunity for learning and establishing effective practitioner-group relationships.

Some children will be resistant to attending the group during the conflict stage; they will say that the group is boring, childish, and that they hate it. Parents need to be counseled that this is a natural phase that some children go through and that their child should continue in the group. Parents who are ambivalent about the relevance or importance of the group experience may allow their child to drop out of the group at this point. This may be damaging to the child by reinforcing fear and a sense of failure. Additionally, the total child must be viewed and not only the acting out behavior. Focusing on irritating externalized behaviors can cause the practitioner to lose sight of the positive aspects of the child.

A major way of resolving the conflict of this stage is to provide activities that are extremely appealing to the children. They tend to abandon their "controlling" behaviors in order to be engaged in the fun, highly motivating activities and in some ways they are "seduced" away from the conflict stage to a commitment towards the group. Participation needs to be structured in such a way that the children do not appear to be giving in. In this process the adult meets the children halfway and does not worry about being right or in charge. In reality the children buy into the group, and the leader's authority is actually enhanced.

Trust and Cohesion

The stage of trust and cohesion is the goal of any social competence group. Therapeutic experiences are designed to establish trust, which allows the children to be comfortable talking and listening, sharing honestly about themselves, and asking for and accepting help. Likewise, activities are provided to facilitate group cohesion, such as a sense of shared ownership and commitment to the group. In this safe and accepting atmosphere, children are free to explore new behaviors including those that evoke uncomfortable feelings such as embarrassment, anger, frustration, and competition. This stage is rather fragile and the group can regress back to the conflict stage; for instance, the addition of a new member, a break in the schedule, or an impending termination of the group can push the group members back into conflict. The trust and cohesion stage is the prime time for the learning, practice, and integration of new social behaviors.

The following activities are excellent for fostering attachment to and acceptance of group members. Trust and cohesion in particular are fostered by participating in constructions, timed team relays, and the creation of life-size portraits.

- **Beanbag walk** — Children are paired. One child walks across the room with a beanbag on his or her head. Each time it falls, the partner picks the beanbag up and places it back on the child's head so that he or she can walk to the goal.

- **Trust walk** — A child closes his or her eyes and is guided by a partner through obstacles or a building.

- **Sharing** — Materials or responsibilities are shared, such as taking different jobs in a cooking activity.

- **Development of group identity** — The children decide collaboratively on a group name, mascot, logo, password, handshake, or opening/closing ritual.

- **Composite drawings** — Children are divided into three pairs to draw a person on a three-sectioned paper. One pair draws the head, another pair draws the chest, and the last pair draws the legs. The group as a whole tells a story about the drawing.

Termination

The last stage of group development is termination. The children are helped to cope with separation from the group and see it as a positive experience. Typically, part of the last three sessions of a 12-week cycle focuses on preparing the children for termination from the group. Often the children, the parents, and the practitioners have feelings that need to be acknowledged. Children may be sad about not seeing their newfound friends on a weekly basis; however, they can continue their friendships after leaving the group. Experiences can also be identified to help generalization of skills and a transition to the child's everyday social life; for instance, the child can be guided toward participation in scouts, soccer, swimming, and after school clubs. Frequently the long-term project has a closing event that provides a natural ending to an intervention cycle; the group can celebrate by having a party, a presentation, or show for the parents and peers. The following activities have been used with documented effectiveness for the termination stage of a group.

- **Review of weekly activities** — Souvenir books and charts can be used as a way of remembering past activities.

- **Memories** — Photographs are taken of the group and audiotapes are made documenting a shared group experience. Each child receives a photo and tape to take home as recorded memories.

- **Rap it up** — Each child evaluates his or her own progress and talks about personal feelings about the group.

- **Warm fuzzies** — Children and adults verbally share positive statements about each other.

Intervention Techniques to Enhance Social Competence

Instructional methods can be divided into direct and indirect techniques (Zeitlin & Williamson, 1994). Indirect intervention strategies influence the child's behavior through management of space, materials, equipment, and the individuals in the surroundings. These strategies set the stage for learning by modifying the environment. Sample indirect strategies include grouping the children together to foster interaction, eliminating environmental distractions for impulsive children, adapting the size and type of play materials, and providing a predictable sequence of activities during intervention for children who have difficulties adjusting to change.

Direct intervention strategies influence the child's behavior through specific interaction with the adult. Traditional teaching techniques and procedures for behavior modification exemplify direct strategies. Sample direct strategies include verbal guidance or coaching to help children solve a task, modeling desired behaviors for the children to imitate, physical prompting to assist performance of an activity, and providing feedback through specific reinforcement schedules.

In most cases, some combination of direct and indirect strategies is required in running effective groups. However, overreliance on direct intervention strategies must be avoided, as this may reinforce an adult orientation and undercut peer socialization. Indirect strategies should be considered for implementation prior to the use of direct strategies; sometimes the slightest modification of an environmental factor, such as regrouping the children, can result in successful social interaction. When environmental modifications do not result in desired behaviors, indirect intervention strategies should be augmented with the use of more direct strategies. This point is particularly true for children who have not acquired fundamental social skills through experience.

In our groups, the following direct intervention strategies have been selectively used. They can be employed during any of the four segments of the group and can be incorporated into an activity orientation instead of conducted as a formal instructional lesson.

For example, a goal was to teach children a number of prosocial skills related to sharing and turn taking. The two adults role-played poor prosocial skills within a construction task of building with blocks. The children, who were shocked and amused at the conduct of the adults, were asked to identify what was wrong in the behaviors. After a discussion, the children were assigned in pairs to the role of coaching one of the adults. As the adults returned to the construction activity, repeating their inappropriate behavior, the children intervened to correct the situation. Gradually, over time, the children took over the construction and the adults faded their involvement as the children demonstrated desired behavior. In this example role-playing, coaching, and teaching were used as direct intervention strategies in a novel and activity-based way.

Direct Teaching

Direct teaching involves instruction in learning a new target behavior and typically includes presenting the rationale for learning the behavior, defining and explaining the topic, demonstrating the behavior, providing opportunities for the child to practice the behavior, and giving feedback about the performance. In the social arena, direct teaching often addresses prosocial skills, communication, and conflict resolution.

The interviewing procedure described in Chapter 13 illustrates the use of direct teaching integrated into an activity. Such instruction can also be implemented in an informal manner rather than in a structured, discrete lesson. For instance, three children are barking orders at each other in the process of building with blocks. The adult intervenes to explain that there is another way to make requests so that others will wish to comply. The adult demonstrates the chosen technique and then practices it with each of the children, who then go back to playing with a new strategy for making requests.

Modeling

Social learning is partly based on the observation and imitation of persons who are meaningful to us; consequently, viewing a desired behavior or skill can be a potent catalyst if the child is interested in the model and able to discern which of the model's behaviors are important. The child needs to identify with the model and admire the model enough to want to imitate the behavior. This principle helps to determine whether the model chosen will be an adult or a child, and once a suitable model is selected, the practitioner points out the specific behaviors that are desirable. Frequently, the practitioner participates as a play partner with the child in selected activities, thus serving as an ongoing informal model. Such a strategy can help a child maintain engagement in a task and explore new play schemes. The use of modeling as a strategy may not work for a child who is not skilled at learning through visual cues.

Role-Playing

In this technique, two or more children perform roles regarding a common experience or problem situation, with the children typically given a specific scenario and roles for each player. Role-playing has the advantage of being highly motivating for most children because they are able to act out different parts in the play. For children with language deficits, role-playing can provide the structure necessary for decreasing anxiety in conversational speech as well as promote the appropriate use of language in interpersonal communication. An atmosphere that provides a safe setting for taking risks is critical to the success of role-playing; some children may be shy and uncertain in the beginning and may need to observe the role-play before participating actively.

Some structured role-plays can target emotionally laden situations, with teasing and bullying being common problem areas. In role-playing, the children practice interactive skills that promote success in stressful situations. While learning targeted prosocial skills, they learn how to be less fearful and more confident. The role-plays can occur naturally at the beginning of the session during conversation time, be introduced during the short-term activity or project activity, or wrap up the session during the closure segment. Topics for emotionally charged role-playing include common problems such as being teased about one's physical appearance or clothing, being ridiculed because one is smart or the teacher's pet, or feeling ostracized because one is new to the school. Other topics include feeling rejected because one is clumsy and uncoordinated, being ignored because one is painfully shy and withdrawn, and falsely assuming that one is being picked on. This latter issue is often a concern of parents.

Another variation on role-playing is the practice of prosocial skills as the children try out new ways of responding with feedback from the practitioner. This form of role-play is particularly meaningful for young children, as each child is able to practice the different parts. Sample prosocial skills include the ability to join ongoing play and the ability to say "no" without hurting the other person's feelings. The role-play can be structured so that two children are engaged in an activity into which a third child wishes to enter. This child can practice ways of asking to join a group, whereas the other two children can role-play acceptance or polite rejection, such as, "Not now, we are almost through," or "Wait a few minutes until we start again." All three children take turns playing each of the roles.

Coaching

Coaching involves direct verbal instruction to a specific child about a specific performance and is provided at the time that the behavior is required. That is, this procedure is implemented within the context of the ongoing action rather than delivered as an isolated instruction session. Coaching provides feedback about a desirable target behavior so that the child will repeat it, and also increases awareness about an undesirable behavior that needs to be stopped or altered. Coaching may also offer instruction regarding steps to achieve a new behavior.

Coaching is particularly effective for the egocentric child who is unaware of his or her undesirable behavioral pattern, such as habitual discounting or a tendency to be bossy and not listen. Coaching is also useful for the child who has poor self-regulation, as the child becomes aware of the hyperaroused behavior and learns to modulate it right when it occurs.

Coaching is an effective vehicle for the acquisition and strengthening of specific skills in the context of daily functioning. At times, feedback should be provided to the child in confidence, possibly taking the child to the side of the room or just outside the door for a private conversation. In addition, coaching can be provided to the child in steps. For example, the practitioner initially provides feedback about the child's specific behavior to establish awareness, and the child begins to recognize that he or she is exhibiting a particular behavior. After a period of time there can be a discussion of the impact of that behavior on others, and eventually the child develops insight regarding what others think of him in response to the behavior. If the child is motivated to develop friends, this coaching procedure can be very successful.

Behavior Management

Any practitioner working in the area of social competence must be well versed in behavior management strategies. These techniques share the operational principle that behavior is strongly influenced by its environmental consequences and is shaped by positive and negative reinforcers. While the breadth of this topic is beyond the scope of this discussion, behavioral concepts are integrated throughout the content of this book, including the theoretical, assessment, and intervention sections.

Peer Tutoring

Peer tutoring involves children helping children, as peers work together with one child functioning in a tutor role and the other in a student role. Peer tutoring often involves modeling, coaching, and direct instruction, and commonly a child with a strong social ability is paired with a child who needs to acquire social skills. The tutor must be carefully chosen and receive specialized training; he or she must be socially skillful, respected by peers, and genuinely interested in the student. A peer tutor can be the same age as the target child or older.

Peer tutoring goes beyond just being buddies, as tutor training and subsequent intervention can address a variety of areas such as learning prosocial skills, conflict resolution, or developing techniques for selling yourself. The student often identifies with the more popular tutor and is motivated to emulate the tutor's behavior, and generalization of new skills is facilitated because skills are being acquired within the student's world of the classroom, the cafeteria, or the playground.

Activity Analysis

At the core of our approach is the strategic use of selected activities for helping children acquire new skills and behaviors. Involvement in shared, age-appropriate, naturalistic activities is a major way that children acquire social competence. Activities must be carefully chosen and graded to be therapeutically employed, and this process requires analysis of the activity's component parts. Activity analysis is the process of examining the multidimensional elements involved in performing any task (Breines, 1995) and enables the practitioner to consider each element independently, as well as in relation to each other and the whole. There are sensory, perceptual, cognitive, and emotional aspects inherent in any activity.

A wide range of activities can be used therapeutically when working in social competence groups or when serving as a practitioner with a particular child. These activities can be adapted and graded to focus on any dimension of the conceptual framework, while the goals of the group determine which aspect of the model is emphasized. Table 12.1 shows how a Monopoly® game can address all components of the conceptual framework; this format is an adapted version of Monopoly that is played in teams of two to three to augment the social nature of the game.

Table 12.1
Therapeutic Potential of Monopoly®

Purpose of Interaction	Instrumental: Asking questions about the game
	Social-emotional: Congratulating team mates on a good move
Social Perspective Taking	Accepting perspectives of others who are interested in buying and selling certain properties
Social and Play Behavior	Knowledge of board games and experience playing on teams
Prosocial Skills	Following rules of the game without cheating
Self-Regulation	Showing patience while waiting turns and managing the shifting fortunes of the game
Communication	Making clear concise statements and asking questions to foster the acquisition of properties
Social Decision Making	Resolving disagreements regarding purchases

Table 12.2 can assist the practitioner in selecting activities by offering a list of play and leisure tasks that have been employed successfully in intervention. The table is organized according to broad functional categories of play.

Table 12.2
Types of Activities

Gross Motor	Verbal	Art
Obstacle courses	Puppet shows and plays	Collages
Relays and races	Charades	Murals
Freeze games (e.g., freeze tag)	Leading an activity	Singing
Follow the leader	Interviewing	Puppetry
Simon Says	Teaching another a skill	Book illustrations
Tag games	Telephone	Mixed media projects
Red light/green light	20 questions	Seasonal projects (e.g., making gifts)

Imaginary Play	Constructions	Miscellaneous
Story telling	Blocks	Celebrations
Playing super heroes	Legos®	Cooking
Puppet show	Playing cards	Community outings
Dress up	Tinker Toys®	Collections
Playing with miniatures	Building models	Challenge course
	Constructing a kite	
	Building a miniature golf course or fort	

Games	
Monopoly®	Strategy and fantasy games
RISK™	Pick-up sticks
Clue®	Jacks
Trivial Pursuit®	Chinese checkers
Puzzles	Dominoes
Tabletop pinball	Ball play
Electronic games	Scavenger and treasure hunts

Engagement in activity is a transaction among the individual (mind and body), the task, and the world (social and physical). Consequently, activity analysis for intervention purposes incorporates four primary factors: the child, the task, the environment, and the practitioner's conscious use of self. For our purposes, activity analysis goes beyond a simple examination of the task itself. The practitioner analyzes each of the four factors and observes their interrelationships in the context of the whole. In order to achieve optimal activity selection and grading, there needs to be a good fit among all of the factors.

To determine appropriate activities, the practitioner needs to consider many aspects of the child's functional performance in context. Sample areas involved in an activity analysis of the child's status include verbal and cognitive ability, interest and motivation, age, gender, cultural background, physical prowess, play history and repertoire, and intervention goals. Sample task characteristics that can be analyzed include adaptability and complexity, opportunities for competition and imaginative expression, age appropriateness, physical properties, and degree of social interaction.

In addition to analysis of the child and the task, the practitioner needs to understand the attributes of the environment. Important aspects include materials and equipment; quality of temperature, air, and lighting; space requirements and limitations; indoor and outdoor options; safety considerations; and degree of distractions. The practitioner must also consider his or her conscious use of self, or the use of oneself in such a way that the practitioner becomes an effective tool in the process of assessment and intervention. In order to interact in such a therapeutic way, the practitioner must have a high degree of self-awareness. Personal traits that can be examined include communication style, personality, social style, degree of empathy, flexibility, and sense of humor and playfulness.

Intervention Process

Intervention planning and implementation involves a six-step process. Variations of this process can be used with individual children or with a group. This approach progresses from initial goal setting through implementation. Figure 12.1 provides an overview of the six steps.

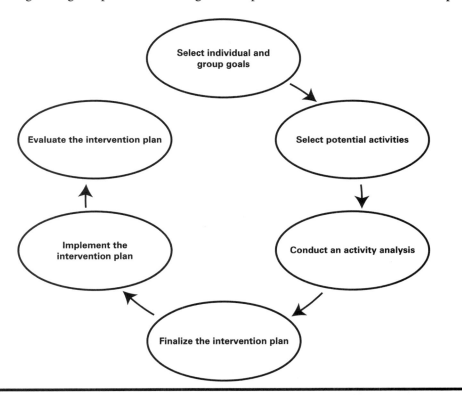

Figure 12.1
Intervention Planning and Implementation

Select Individual and Group Goals

In this step the practitioner follows the guidelines described in Chapter 9 regarding goal setting, which may be considered the bridge between assessment and intervention. Individual goals are established for each child, and then group goals are synthesized from this group profile. During this step, the individual and group goals emerge from the conceptual framework.

Select Potential Activities

A list of potential activities that are age appropriate and relevant to the intervention goals are chosen. With these goals and the conceptual framework in mind, the practitioner can peruse Table 12.2 for ideas. The following guidelines are useful for relating different aspects of the model to activity selection.

Social Perspective Taking

Egocentrism of the children is of primary concern because narcissism colors all other aspects of social functioning. Therefore, the degree of egocentricity must be considered before addressing other social issues. Problems in perspective taking interfere with social decision making, reciprocal communication skills, and the ability to self-regulate because of noncompliance or challenging rules. A child with a high degree of egocentrism is unable to de-center from a self-oriented vantage point. Therefore, activities need to be chosen that require the generation of numerous ideas and problem solving from various viewpoints and that further provide numerous alternatives and solutions rather than a single, black and white outcome. For example, in the execution of a group construction task there is ample opportunity for negotiation and give and take regarding the final product and the steps to achieve it.

Social and Play Behavior

Gross motor activities and games are excellent tools for addressing problems in social and play behavior. Special attention needs to be given to the age and skill levels of the children and their peer-related culture. Many children have a severely limited play repertoire and perseverate in following one or two activities. The key is to introduce a wide array of activities that expands the children's interests; such activities need to be enticing and fun, and should lead to a successful outcome for all of the children involved. However, this guideline does not pertain to children who have a strong interest and talent in a particular domain and therefore pursue it with vigor.

Prosocial Skills

Intervention to address prosocial skills can highlight verbal activities, imaginary play, and board games. All of these activities foster such prosocial skills as sharing, turn taking, requesting, following rules, and negotiating conflict.

Self-Regulation

Gross motor activities that have an element of "start and stop" are excellent for self-regulation of the body. Board games also emphasize self-regulation because they are rule-governed but include having to manage the fortunes of luck. In addition, unstructured activities such as constructions, art, and imaginary play require flexible thinking and are helpful for improving cognitive self-monitoring.

Communication

There are a variety of verbal activities that emphasize self-expression, comprehension, and memory, including interviewing, teaching or story telling. A child can be placed in a leadership role in which he or she has to direct others within the chosen activity. Special attention needs to be placed on pragmatics, discourse skills, and nonverbal communication.

Social Decision Making

Intervention activities are designed to achieve a goal while working with partners or a small group. Constructions and gross motor activities lend themselves to fostering social decision-making. Most activities from Monopoly to making collages can be adapted to incorporate active problem solving. Now that the practitioner has identified a number of activities that have therapeutic and educational potential for addressing targeted goals, the next step is to perform an analysis of these activities in order to make a final selection.

Conduct an Activity Analysis

The practitioner now examines each of the potential activities according to their attributes related to the child, the task, the environment, and the practitioner's conscious use of self. Table 12.3 provides questions that consider each of these elements in the activity analysis. These questions help the practitioner to select one or more appropriate activities and to grade them according to the needs of the group.

Typically, practitioners are most skilled at conducting an activity analysis when it is focused on an individual and not a group; likewise, they are most apt to emphasize successful task completion and not the social and interactive group process. The challenge is to identify activities that foster social cohesion in a heterogeneous collection of individuals. The practitioner needs to create a situation in which each child can spontaneously be social and interactive without being distracted by the concrete demands of the task. If the activity is too hard, the children will not interact socially due to an intense focus on performing the task. The activity analysis of inexperienced practitioners tends to focus too much on the specific steps of the activity because the children have such varied skill levels, and as a result one loses sight of the potential of the activity as a catalyst for social engagement. One common mistake made by seasoned practitioners is to assume that they are knowledgeable about the activity and fail to do a complete analysis with these particular children in mind. The more familiar the activity, the more likely a practitioner is to conduct a hasty analysis and make a mistake.

The selection and grading of therapeutic tasks is based on a thorough activity analysis. The practitioner needs to be sure that the activity can occur over an adequate number of sessions so that there is ample time for evolution of the social interaction, as some tasks do not allow for natural extension and are completed too quickly. Likewise, the cognitive and language demands of the task must match the children's level of capability. Of special importance is the analysis of the receptive language, expressive language, and processing demands of the tasks. Should observed behaviors make it necessary to grade down the activity to a more simplistic level, the practitioner must be careful not to infantilize the children. For instance, the practitioner should adapt the board game of Sorry!® to accommodate varied language and cognitive abilities, rather than to abandoning its use for that of Candy Land®, which is appropriate for younger children.

Table 12.3
Guidelines For Activity Analysis

Child Considerations

Is the activity appropriate for the child's developmental play level? (e.g., onlooker, parallel, associative, or cooperative stage)

Does the child have the verbal and motor skills needed to accomplish the task?

What cognitive level is required? (e.g., concrete versus abstract thinking)

Is the activity appropriate for the child's sex, age, and cultural background?

Will the child be able to engage in the task if modifications are provided?

Task Considerations

How complex is the task? Can it be divided into small, sequential steps?

How much preparation is necessary?

How long does the task take for completion? (e.g., one versus multiple sessions)

How excitable is the task? Does it tend to stimulate or calm the child's energy and activity levels?

How much practice and repetition does the task allow?

Does the activity provide an opportunity for physical and emotional release?

Is it a no-fail task or one that has specific criteria for judging success?

Is the activity interesting and motivating?

What is the degree to which fantasy or creative expression is permitted or encouraged?

Does the activity result in a finished product? Is it an individual or group product?

What is the degree of structure required? (e.g., number of concrete rules and options for making choices)

How competitive is the activity?

What level of cooperation is necessary or allowed? How interdependent and reciprocal is the play? How much does one child's action directly affect another child's response?

How much opportunity is provided for informal and spontaneous social exchange such as chatting during snack time or "kibitzing" during games?

Does the activity allow for a variety of ways to group the children? (e.g., solitary, dyads, triads, small or large group)

What are the motoric demands of the activity? How can they be graded?

How much time is required for each phase of the activity?

Environmental Considerations

Is there adequate space to conduct and store the activity?

Are the lighting and temperature adequate for the group?

What are the environmental requirements of the activity?

Can the task be performed indoors and outdoors?

What is the degree of environmental distractibility? (e.g., visual, auditory, olfactory)

Table 12.3 (*continued*)

Considerations Regarding Conscious Use of Self

What is the practitioner's role in the activity itself?

How do activity requirements match the attributes and characteristics of the practitioner?

Is the practitioner playful?

Is the practitioner empathic to the specific emotional issues of the children and their families?

How much help or assistance does the practitioner need to provide in order to facilitate success?

Is the practitioner able to understand the "scenario" from the perspective of each participant? (e.g., appreciating a tag activity from the vantage point of a shy child and a gregarious child)

How much encouragement and feedback does the practitioner need to provide to individual participants and the group as a whole?

How can the practitioner encourage altruistic behavior in the group (e.g., encouraging the participants to notice the need for help and offering it)?

Practitioners need to analyze the activity from varied perspectives so that they are aware of multiple ways to facilitate the task. Through this perspective taking they can anticipate the divergent responses of the children. Preparation for an activity involves assembling the required tools and materials, practicing the task until its component elements are well understood, and rehearsing varied ways to communicate the directions. Being able to adapt activities enables the practitioner to make choices that are age appropriate as well as currently popular with children.

The environment can promote or interfere with the play behavior of children in numerous ways (Knox & Mailloux, 1997). Contextual factors that foster play include availability of people and objects, freedom from stress, opportunities for repetition and choice, novelty, and space for exploration. The factors that inhibit play include excessive challenge and competition, external constraints, too much novelty, self-consciousness, limiting choices by stereotyping the children, and under- and overstimulation. Whereas many are addressed while analyzing the task, these factors must be revisited when analyzing the environment, as the task and the environment are interrelated and influence each other. An activity analysis focused solely on the task separate from the environmental context will be artificial and incomplete.

Consider the following illustration. Sam, a group leader of Scout Troop 16, planned a ball activity to promote physical exercise and team spirit. In his activity analysis Sam considered the steps of the task, allocation of roles, directions to follow, and length of time to play. He failed to consider the major environmental factor that was the influence of playing outside on the playground. Once on the field, the boys were totally distracted by the noise, wind, and open space; the sensory stimulation and lack of physical boundaries caused them to exhibit disorganized and rowdy behavior. Sam failed to appreciate the transaction between the task and the environment in his preparation.

A critical aspect of activity analysis is the introspection that allows for the conscious or therapeutic use of self. The practitioner's personal feelings about each child and family will influence the therapeutic relationship. Every practitioner has emotional reactions and biases of one kind or another; he or she must be conscious of these feelings and manage them in such a way as to be able to develop an alliance with the other individuals. For example, a young adolescent named Katrina has a social problem related to being extremely overweight. Her mother is also obese and did not provide consistent support to Katrina regarding weight loss. The therapist has a strong reaction against the mother for undercutting Katrina's progress. In this example the therapist must manage her personal feelings and reactions in order to counsel Katrina and her mother effectively.

In another case, Diane intentionally manipulated other children and made cutting remarks to them. Her teacher, Ms. Benson, was offended by this behavior, becoming angry with Diane. Ms. Benson found herself responding to Diane in an impatient and irritated way, even when such a reaction was not warranted. When a teaching assistant commented on her behavior, Ms. Benson became aware of her attitude and came to realize that she needed to look beyond Diane's presenting behavior to possible causes. She was embarrassed that she had lost her professional composure and had developed a negative attitude toward one of her students. She was then now able to develop an alliance with Diane that was free of undercurrents and unconscious agendas.

One of the most challenging aspects regarding the conscious use of self is the demeanor that one assumes when interacting with children. Although interaction during play should be spontaneous and fun, the practitioner has an additional role of being developmental and therapeutic. The practitioner assumes a stage role instead of being his- or herself as reflected in personal life. The execution of this role is guided by therapeutic objectives and must appear natural in order to be effective. Posturing and an artificial attitude are inadvisable, as the practitioner must appear genuinely engaged and not fake. This functioning on two tracks, both being engaged with the children in a spontaneous way while facilitating the group dynamics, requires expertise and the conscious use of self.

All practitioners have a personal history regarding their use of activities. They have strengths and weaknesses in their activity repertoire that influence their preferences and attitudes. Practitioners need to be aware of these preferences and how they can influence activity selection. For instance, an occupational therapist may tend to overuse sensorimotor or art activities and avoid language or communication activities. Conversely, a speech-language pathologist may prefer language activities and avoid sensorimotor tasks. The practitioner's comfort with competition also affects activity choice. Practitioners who are extremely competitive may automatically build competition into all aspects of group activities, while those who are uncomfortable with competition may design activities so that there is never a winner or loser. Both of these extremes are unhelpful because children need to learn to manage competitive situations at developmentally appropriate levels. These illustrations show the importance of involving the conscious use of self in the activity analysis process.

Thus, the activity analysis is completed on one or more planned activities. The activity is analyzed from the perspective of the child, the task, the environment, and the conscious use of self. By conducting an activity analysis, the practitioner has selected the activities for the group, has an awareness of how to present the activities, and has identified strategies for grading and modifying them. The practitioner is now ready to formulate the final plan.

Finalize the Intervention Plan

During this step in the therapeutic use of activity, the practitioner makes detailed plans for intervention that are reminiscent of a teacher's lesson plan. This plan includes the specifics for implementation — who, what, when, where, and how. The practitioner plans to introduce the activity in a motivating way, to present goals of the activity in child-friendly terms, and to provide directions and rules for participation in the activity. The practitioner will find it advisable to design at least three different modifications for implementing this blueprint, as all practitioners occasionally face circumstances in which carefully constructed plans fail; attendance may be poor, the children may be unresponsive, or the therapist may have miscalculated the abilities of the children. Any or all of these circumstances might necessitate a change in the activity. During planning, the practitioner should consider how individual children may respond to the activity, and therefore be prepared for a variety of idiosyncratic responses that might occur.

There are several other important factors to be addressed in finalizing the intervention plan. The environment is a crucial factor, and the practitioner must determine how to prepare the environment and space for the group experience. Time is also a critical factor, as the period of time a group is together needs to have a rhythm and balanced pace as the children move from one activity to another. Each activity requires adequate time devoted to group process, skill acquisition, and practice. Activities need to last long enough to be meaningful without becoming boring. Other practical considerations need to be addressed such as the storage of materials, supplies, and created constructions. Finally, the practitioner may consider different ways for parents or other adults to be involved in the activity when it is appropriate.

Implement the Plan

Now that the practitioner has a well-defined plan of action, the intervention plan may require the practitioner to assume a number of roles ranging from program planner to direct service provider. For example, the practitioner may be involved in one-to-one therapy, consultation with parents and classroom personnel, conducting a social competence group, or participation in a community-based recreational program. Regardless of the roles played, the quality of the activity analysis will be crucial to successful intervention. This analysis allows spontaneous adaptations of the tasks as required, or in some cases the abandonment of particular activities that are not achieving the therapeutic goal.

During the implementation stage, the practitioner has responsibility for specific children, tasks, and materials. In addition, the practitioner must pay attention to other multiple events, such as the flow of the session, group dynamics, and tracking of time. In many ways this is the most demanding aspect of conducting social competence groups — managing the conscious use of self in the context of multiple demands. During the flow of the session the practitioner must decide how and if to continue the activity, how to manage disruptions, and when to stop.

The following illustration depicts the complexity of managing these multiple demands. In a new social competence group, each child was given the assignment of interviewing another member of the group, thus forming five pairs. The task was defined as each child taking turns interviewing his or her partner in much the same way as people chat to get to know each other. After a period of time the children were to report back to the entire group what each had learned about the new friend. Two practitioners monitored the five pairs during the interviews. One practitioner noticed that in one of her pairs, the interviewer was becoming increasingly silly, and as a result the interviewee was becoming grandiose and untruthful in his statements. In another pair, the interviewer was having difficulty asking questions, and the interviewee was giving a monologue, while in a third pair the conversation had gone off-topic into a discussion about how to play the latest Game Boy®, a popular electronic toy. The challenge to the practitioner was to provide selective intervention to each of the pairs to get them back on track while monitoring the group as a whole. The effectiveness of the practitioner in conducting this intervention is dependent upon the thoroughness of the activity analysis.

Evaluate the Intervention Plan

Throughout the implementation phase, the practitioner is evaluating the success and effectiveness of the plan, and activities are modified or replaced depending upon the practitioner's judgment. An activity can be evaluated as it unfolds, at the end of a session, at the conclusion of a series of sessions, or upon completion of the activity over time. The practitioner can adapt the intervention plan at any point. For example, the intervention plan may be hastily reformulated if the discussion during circle time reveals an unexpected interest among several group members. If the new topic lends itself to meeting the individual and group goals, the practitioner can follow the children's lead by building upon their strengths and motivation. To achieve this, the practitioner must conduct a complete activity analysis on the new interest, and an experienced practitioner can often perform this analysis on the spot in his or her head.

On occasion, a more formal evaluation of the intervention plan may be warranted. The individual and group goals are reviewed to determine the degree to which they have been accomplished: that is, whether each goal has been achieved, partially achieved, or unattained. Also, the goals are analyzed regarding whether they are appropriate and functionally relevant. Each of the chosen activities is assessed for its value in fostering goal attainment. The practitioner also evaluates how he or she contributed to the therapeutic process.

The outcome of the evaluation process is twofold: to revise the intervention plan for the current group of children, and to expand understanding of particular activities and their use for future intervention. At the end of this final step of evaluation, the cycle begins again on the six-step approach to the therapeutic use of activity.

Illustration

The following example illustrates the six-step process for intervention planning and implementation with an emphasis on activity analysis (i.e., Figure 12.1). The seven children in this example were 6 to 7 years old, attending first-grade classes at a large elementary school, and experiencing problems related to language delays, attention difficulties, and learning disabilities. Once a week these children attended the social competence group ("the club"), which was co-directed by an occupational therapist and the physical education teaching assistant.

Select Individual and Group Goals

The individual goals for the children included:

1. Expand their play repertoire, both social and play behavior;

2. Increase comfort when playing with others; and

3. Enhance communication to get personal needs met.

Two primary group goals identified are:

1. Increase the ability to work on shared activities for up to 10 minutes; and

2. Accept ideas and suggestions of others some of the time.

These goals promote the social skills necessary for cooperative learning and are therefore educationally relevant.

Select Potential Activities

Of the types of activities listed in Table 12.2, the group leaders decided that construction activities were ideally suited to address the individual and group goals. Shared constructions require cooperative play, communication, and collaboration to be successful, and this type of activity has a tremendous capacity for therapeutic grading and modification according to the needs of the children.

Conduct an Activity Analysis

The analysis examined specific construction activities from the perspective of the child, the task, the environment, and the practitioner's conscious use of self. The group of seven children was divided into two subgroups based on their functional ability.

Child Group A: Half of the children enjoy and are skilled in constructions but want to be in charge and do not like taking directions.

Group B: Half of the children are poor in constructions and communication skills.

Task Group A: The task needs to be challenging because the children have substantial experience and skills. Novelty could be achieved by using unfamiliar materials or combining familiar ones that are rarely used together. The challenge could be enhanced by requiring the group to make the tallest, widest, or longest structure possible.

Group B: To ensure a successful end product, one needed to make low demands for preplanning and fine motor control while providing a high degree of structure. The therapist must guarantee that the end product of Group B is as interesting in appearance as the end product for Group A. Despite their limitations in skills, the children of Group B need to produce a structure that does not look second rate or childish.

Environment The environment needs to be uncluttered with the two groups spread apart so that they can work independently.

Group A: To facilitate interaction, visual boundaries are needed for the structure (e.g., mat, poster board, cardboard). The confined space encourages the children to work together and share ideas.

Group B: The practitioner offers optimal structure for these children by distributing materials in containers (according to color, size, and shape) and providing directions on where and how to begin.

Conscious Use of Self Group A: The practitioners serve as resource persons and coaches to remind the children of the rules. The adults monitor the activity without being too intrusive.

Group B: The practitioners serve as models for the construction. The adults gradually shift from directing the activity to playing a supportive role.

Finalize the Intervention Plan

The intervention plan had separate strategies for carrying out the construction activity for the two groups.

Group A

The practitioner provides the following directions: "Choose together what you are going to make. It must be one structure with lots of windows. You must use materials from all of the containers. Before you start, check out the materials." Previewing the materials is a prime motivator and generates enthusiasm for the activity. The children will hopefully jointly identify their desired end product and start construction, with any necessary coaching from the adults. The practitioners should remind the children of their expectations for desired behavior by making statements such as, "Offer ideas and listen to those of others" and "Do not undo someone else's work."

The practitioner must remember to follow the lead of the children. Repeated collapse and failure of the construction actually motivates the group as they "figure out" how to make it work.

Group B

Each child is given an identical set of interesting materials of different objects, shapes, and colors. The practitioners provide the following directions: "Watch what I do and copy me." A practitioner begins by placing a large object in the center of the mat, and then places a non-matching piece next to it. The practitioner then asks the group, "Who has one like this one?" while indicating the second piece. All of the children should answer affirmatively because they have identical sets. Then the practitioners decide who goes next. That child should place a matching piece on top of, or next to, its mate. Now a new piece is added, the same question is posed to the group. The practitioner begins to fade the cueing as soon as the children gradually learn the rules, and the routine continues until all the pieces are used up.

Implement the Intervention Plan

Before reaching this step, individual and group goals were determined, activities were selected and analyzed, and the intervention plan was finalized. In this step, the children engage in the construction activity until completion. The children in Group A had the challenge of constructing one structure. Therefore they had to think creatively, convince others of the desirability of their ideas, relinquish preferences that were unsupported, and blend ideas with those of others.

Initially, all Group A members attempted to impose their own plans on each other. The intensity of this self-advocacy was high. With gentle reminders of the goals and rules from the adults, the participants tried again to develop one plan and begin work. However, several individual structures were started with accompanying rationales such as, "We can join them in the end!" The practitioners calmly dismantled all the work, forcing everyone to focus on the rules anew. As the group process developed over time, collaboration emerged. One child was a "hold out," insisting on his own ideas and whining that no one was listening. He never quite made it into the group process, even after numerous overtures from group members.

The construction task for Group B was structured, involving imitation to learn all aspects of the activity. The children required repetition and practice to become familiar and comfortable with the materials and the construction process. Constant reminders about turn taking were necessary because the children all wanted to act at once. Their first attempt resulted in a too-tall structure that collapsed. As a result the children began to be more careful in their building design, and the resulting construction had a horizontal base to support its vertical towers. In general, there was a smoother flow from one child to another as they proceeded through the steps of the task.

Evaluate the Intervention Plan

The occupational therapist and the physical education teaching assistant reviewed the group process. They had anticipated that the children in Group A would function independently and try to impose their ideas on others, but the intervention strategy of gentle reminders was not robust enough to alter these behaviors. The physical strategy of halting the work and removing the materials was required to gain the children's attention and reinforce the need for one construction. All of the children responded to the intervention except for one boy who held rigidly to his original plan. Knowing the child, the therapist considered his behavior a reflection of his attentional problems. The child was unable to consider simultaneously his own thoughts and those of others, and he felt that he must insist on his own plan of operation or completely sacrifice his own ideas for those of his peers. The possibility of combining ideas was unattainable for him because it required joint attention to several ideas at once.

In evaluating the intervention plan for Group A, the goals and activity choice were considered appropriate as reflected in the successful and enthusiastic participation of the children. The next phase was to allow them to implement more elaborate ideas with the same activity now that they were familiar with each other. The only change was to have the child who was disengaged have more control in determining the first part of the construction; the more formal role helped decrease his anxiety and facilitated flexibility and participation.

The individual and group goals for Group B were considered on target. The activity choice and its structure were successful with the children. Although the repetition regarding the rules was anticipated, the therapist was surprised that the children were so naive regarding the materials, demonstrating inattention to the properties and details of the materials. This limitation in skill probably reflected inexperience and lack of practice secondary to their learning disabilities. The next phase of the intervention plan provided more sessions of the same activity with progressively more varied and interesting materials. This strategy allowed the children to practice their targeted skills while maintaining high motivation.

This example illustrates how practitioners can follow the six-step process for intervention planning and implementation in the context of a social competence group. In the beginning of a group, each step is highlighted. After cycling through the steps over time, the emphasis on individual steps begins to vary. For instance, if the group has made gains but goals remain unchanged, the practitioner may need to identify new activities and then analyze their components. During a social competence group that runs for four months, the six-step process will be used numerous times.

The six-step intervention planning process can be complex and time consuming, particularly in the early stage of learning it. With time and practice, however, the process becomes increasingly automatic and efficient. Competence in activity analysis requires an initial investment of effort but is the key to meaningful intervention. Respect for the therapeutic use of activity is at the heart of our approach. With experience, the practitioner has an increasing repertoire of previously analyzed activities that can be readily implemented in practice, and ultimately, the practitioner will accumulate a roster of activities that can be selectively used in his or her group work. These activities require only a brief review, whereas unfamiliar or new ones will require a more in-depth analysis.

Sample Activities

Almost any activity, if carefully designed and graded, can be therapeutically employed to enhance social skills. The activities described in this chapter have been used and refined in social competence groups over a period of 15 years and have been used successfully to achieve individual and group goals. The sample activities are diverse, age appropriate, highly motivating, and gender neutral. They are categorized according to type — gross motor, art, constructions, games, verbal, imaginary play, and miscellaneous. The purpose of each activity is discussed, a description is provided of the most common approach to the activity, environmental requirements are delineated, and potential modifications are offered.

Table 13.1 lists these activities according to the conceptual framework discussed in Section 2. Activity options are listed in the activity selection column. For example, there are eight major activities, each with a number of modifications, listed in the gross motor section. The practitioner can choose an activity and then read across the row to determine the major therapeutic benefit according to the conceptual framework. For instance, floor puzzles in the Game section primarily benefit the facilitation of perspective taking and social and play behavior. Practitioners may add new activities to this roster over time and thus expand their own therapeutic repertoire.

Table 13.1
Activities According to the Conceptual Framework

Activity Selection		Perspective Taking	Instrumental Interaction	Social-Emotional Interaction	Social & Play Behavior	Prosocial Skills	Self-Regulation	Communication	Social Decision Making
Gross Motor	The "Glob"						●		
	Cooperative Musical Chairs				●		●		
	Beanbag Juggling				●		●		
	Red Light Green Light						●	●	
	Statues						●	●	
	Parachute				●		●		
	Relays				●	●	●		
	Obstacle Course				●	●	●		
Art	Wallpaper				●				
	Collages	●	●		●	●	●	●	●
	Life-sized Portraits	●		●		●			
	Musical Activities				●		●	●	
	Puppetry							●	●
Constructions	Wooden Sculpture				●	●			
	Building With Blocks	●			●	●			●
Games	Floor Puzzles	●		●					
	Ball Play				●	●	●		
	Scavenger Hunt				●		●	●	●
	Life Sized Monopoly					●	●	●	●
Verbal	Interviewing	●	●	●				●	
	Bop-It				●		●	●	
	"Where's Waldo?"		●					●	
	Quiz Show	●	●	●			●	●	
	Who Am I?	●	●					●	
	Video Role Play				●		●	●	●
Imaginary Play	Mime Phrases							●	
	Storytelling	●		●				●	●
Miscellaneous	Collecting				●	●		●	
	Celebrations	●		●	●	●	●		
	Long-term, Complex Projects	●	●	●	●	●	●	●	●

Gross Motor Activities

The Glob

Purpose

This activity, which helps children practice self-regulation, requires a start-stop repetition. The children must modulate their excitability despite the arousing tempo, and the task involves touching and physical proximity.

Description

This is a modified tag game with the goal of all of the children joining hands creating the "Glob." It begins with two children holding hands in a circle and acting as the initial Glob. They run after the other children until one is tagged; then that child joins the other two in the Glob. This activity is repeated until all the children are touched and become part of the Glob.

The job of the children composing the Glob is to capture everyone in the group one at a time; the job of the other children is to run around and avoid capture. All the children are ultimately part of the Glob and experience a sense of group cohesion. Indeed, the end of the game may be celebrated by all of the children in a circle throwing their hands in the air and shouting, "Go Glob!"

The activity requires no set up except an open space and can be completed in 10–15 minutes. This game is excellent for children who are developmentally low functioning as well as for children with good skills, but it is contraindicated for children who exhibit major signs of tactile defensiveness or who are easily overwhelmed. The game can be used for children up to age 12.

Environment/Materials

The intent of this game is to be noisy, fun, and thrilling; it requires space for running and noise making.

Modification

There are two primary ways to increase the complexity of the game to require greater modulation of activity level and emotional arousal; the children will become increasingly more organized and less random in their behavior. In the first variation, each child has a sticker with a different color placed on his or her back. The group leader identifies a color that should be tagged, and the two children who are the Glob must race around the room trying to locate the identified color. When it is located, that person is captured and becomes part of the Glob. The group leader then identifies another color and the searching continues by the Glob. This process is repeated until all children are a part of the Glob. In the second variation, the method of tagging is changed, to be more demanding by requiring the Glob to encircle each child with its arms while not letting go of hand holding.

Cooperative Musical Chairs

Purpose

This activity teaches self-regulation because it requires the children to monitor their activity levels in a stop-and-go fashion. It is also helpful for expanding the play repertoire of children, particularly those who need to be more playful and less serious.

Description

Children march to music around chairs that face out in a circle. When the music stops, each finds a chair on which to sit. One chair is removed each time the music stops; thus, each child must find a chair to sit on by sharing chairs with others. In contrast to the traditional, competitive game, the chairs are eliminated rather than the children. At the end of the game, several children are sitting precariously on each chair with joyous glee and laughter.

This activity is a variant on a standard party game and is therefore age appropriate for a wide variety of children. The cooperative version ensures that everybody wins and results in an emotional tone of shared joy. However, some children have difficulty adjusting to the new rules and protest that they prefer to play the real way.

Environment/Materials

A large space is required for the circle of chairs, plus room for the children to move around it. A tape recorder or compact disc player can supply music. This activity is exciting and tends to be noisy.

Modifications

A major variation to make the activity easier and to grade the required physical contact is to use carpet samples instead of chairs. The participants play the game standing and do not sit. Instead of carpet samples, the floor can be marked with colored paper, paper plates, or even masking tape strips. When the music stops, the children have progressively fewer markers on which to stand, using one or both feet depending upon the chosen rule.

To make the activity more demanding, a variety of seating possibilities may be used, such as large balls, bolsters, T-stools, or chairs of different heights. This diversity of seating places different types of balance and coordination demands on the children. Seating devices may be removed at random during the game, or the practitioner may intentionally remove the most stable first, so that the sitting equipment with the maximum physical challenge is removed last.

The music selection influences the arousal of the children; for example, a vigorous rock song energizes the children and increases the intensity of the game. The practitioners grade the tempo of the music and its volume to regulate the activity level of the children.

Beanbag Juggling

Purpose

This activity stresses rapidly shifting visual attention, simultaneous attention to different motor demands, and coordination of effort between two or more players. A great sense of mastery and accomplishment develops when juggling effectively in unison. This activity also provides preparation for ball activities and sports, which adds to the child's play repertoire.

Description

The activity begins as a simple toss of one beanbag between two players standing a few feet away from one another, which serves as a warm-up while the children learn to coordinate movements with a partner. After this practice is completed, each child takes his beanbag and tosses it in synchrony to the partner. They organize their timing to match one another by saying "One, two, three, throw!" and with this cue they toss the beanbags at the same time. One partner can have the responsibility for counting the number of successful tosses that have occurred. The next step is to add a third child, creating a **three-way** toss that is more like juggling. The three **players** should follow the cue of "One, two, three, throw!" to establish a regular rhythm.

Environment/Materials

Ample space is required for the partners to be as far apart as skill level will allow.

Modification

This activity can be graded in level of complexity to accommodate players with a range of skills. Even children with poor motor skills can be successful at this task and feel a sense of pride at approximating juggling. A number of pairs or trios can operate at different levels of challenge during this activity. The number of people participating in the group can easily be increased. You can increase complexity by increasing the distance between the participants or varying the objects that are thrown; choices include beanbags, balls, or plastic bowling pins. You can increase the difficulty level by using objects dissimilar in size, shape, or weight, for example, tossing a small throw pillow and a 4-pound medicine ball. The children can also be invited to think up unique ways for making the game more challenging. There are many possibilities including making the object spin in flight, clapping after throwing the object, or turning in place before catching the object.

Red Light, Green Light

Purpose

This gross motor activity targets listening skills, regulation of arousal, and motor activity.

Description

Children are lined up facing a leader who is turned away from them. The leader says "green light" and the children start moving quickly toward him. The leader then says "red light," indicating that the other children should stop immediately and completely. Upon saying "red light," the leader turns around to identify any child who is caught still moving; if caught, a child must return to the starting line. The game is over when one child reaches the leader. This is a highly exciting game that challenges the children to modulate their activity level. The start-stop nature of the game enables the children to practice self-monitoring. This game works well for pre-school and early elementary school children.

Environment/Materials

The game requires a large open area such as a gym, long hallway, or large room.

Modifications

The game can be upgraded to require the players to function in teams of two or three. The rules are kept consistent, but all team members must reach the leader before a winner is declared. You can increase the level of motor difficulty by having the children play on their knees, carry an object, or move backward toward the leader.

Statues

Purpose

The goals of this activity are to promote behavioral regulation and attention to body language.

Description

Children move or dance independently to music. When the music stops, each "freezes like a statue," maintaining the posture he or she was in when the music stopped. The posture is often precarious because the children were in mid-movement. The start-stop quality of the activity challenges self-regulation and motor control. Next the practitioner chooses one child for the children to imitate his or her posture. This task requires the children to read the body language of another child, involving the use of social perception, and assume it. The children must be precise in copying the posture and facial expression of the designated child. This activity is appropriate for children ages 4–9 and is often used with children exhibiting hyperarousal such as hyperactivity, impulsivity, and distractibility.

Environment/Materials

This activity requires space for the children to be free to move and dance. A tape recorder or compact disc player provides the music.

Modifications

The game can be made more exciting, and therefore more stimulating, by loudly playing fast and upbeat music. On the other hand soft music tends to inhibit the arousal level. You can modify the motor excitability of the children by having them dance on carpet samples, which provides the children with a sense of spatial boundaries. Part of the skill in conducting this activity is balancing the level of arousal that is encouraged while insuring that the children can maintain and manage their self-control.

Parachute

Purpose

Popular because it can focus on many goals, the parachute task promotes self-regulation of arousal and attention, motor control and endurance, coordination of effort with others, sensory processing, and joy with peers. This activity should be used with caution for children who are highly sensitive to touch or become easily hyperaroused.

Description

Commercially available "parachutes" can be obtained from recreation and athletic supply sources or medical rehabilitation catalogs. However, real parachutes are preferred because the fabric is softer and not a stiff nylon. You can control the size of a real parachute by rolling up the edges until the circle is small enough for the group and the available space. Participants then hold on to the parachute by gripping the roll. Typically, the parachute is laid out in a circle and the participants are distributed equally around it. They can hold the parachute in a circle while sitting, kneeling or standing. The parachute can be used effectively with young children through adolescents; for younger children or a smaller area, a bed sheet can substitute for the parachute.

There are numerous ways to manipulate the parachute to create different shapes and experiences. There is a joyous magic in seeing the fabric billow in the air and assume changing forms. No one individual can make this happen; it must be a shared experience.

Several activities can be done with a parachute. While standing in a circle holding the parachute, participants raise their arms up to create a dome. With the parachute in the overhead dome position, specific children are asked to change sides before the dome collapses, and the designated children scurry furiously to find spots on the other side. From the dome position, the parachute can be lowered behind the children's backs, and they then sit on the edge of it; the fabric stretched over the heads of all the participants creates the illusion of an igloo. Another option is to ask the children to kneel in a circle and then flutter the parachute so that it billows or flaps; while it is billowing, selected children can either crawl under it or walk barefoot on it.

Environment/Materials

Ideally a large, empty space is used indoors or outdoors for this group activity.

Modifications

There are a number of possible variations on the use of the parachute to promote particular therapeutic and social outcomes. Standing in the periphery of the circle holding the parachute, the children gently raise and lower it while attempting to keep objects such as balloons, beach balls, beanbags, or small throw pillows on the parachute. As the children flap the parachute, the objects bounce around on its surface, while the children excitedly work together to prevent the objects from flying off the parachute. This experience helps the children to shift from an egocentric orientation to the perspective of the group as a whole.

To play a variation called the "Shark" game, the children sit in a large circle on the floor surrounding the open parachute. The adult chooses a child to be the first shark to hunt for prey. The shark crawls under the parachute while the rest of the children make waves with it. Under the parachute the shark "attacks" the legs of a child, and this child becomes the new shark. The game continues until each child gets a turn to be the shark.

The cocoon modification starts by having the parachute in a circle on the floor with the standing children distributed equally around it. Two children are asked to sit back-to-back in the middle of the parachute. The remaining children slowly walk around the circle holding the edge of the parachute. As they walk, the parachute gently wraps the seated children in a "cocoon," gradually bringing the children closer to those seated. Some children like to have the final few feet of the parachute draped over their heads, while others prefer to keep their heads exposed. Once the cocoon is complete, the group members talk to the wrapped children to check on how they feel. Then they begin to reverse the process, slowly unwrapping the seated children. This modification helps the group members to focus on the emotional state of the seated children.

Relays

Purpose

This activity enhances cooperative play, self-regulation, and prosocial skills such as following rules. Relays are highly enjoyable and foster fun interaction. Careful planning of these activities makes it possible for children with a wide range of motor skills to play together, reinforcing confidence and self-esteem.

Description

Relays are familiar activities, commonly played in school, and many variations can be enjoyed. Typically, two or more teams with two or more members compete. Often the structure for the relay is to have the children lined up on one side of a playing area with a target on the other side. The first child of each team runs to the target, touches it, and returns to tap the next teammate. That child then runs the lap and returns to tap the next child. This pattern repeats until all team members have had a chance to participate, and the team that finishes first wins.

Environment/Materials

This activity can be played inside or outside as long as the space is large enough to accommodate the run. Hallways can be considered if a gym or playground is not available. For children who are under age nine, a room that is 20 feet square is acceptable. Because team spirits are high, relays are very noisy.

Modifications

The relay can be modified by the mode of locomotion; walking, running, crawling, moving in a crab walk, walking backward, riding a scooter board, or being pulled on a scooter board are all possibilities, with the choice of locomotion depending on the therapeutic goal to be addressed and the preference of the children. Another variation is to have the team divided so that half of the team is on one side and the other team members are on the opposite side. In this way each child in turn runs half the distance of the previously described pattern. In a common variation, the runner carries an object and hands it off to the next runner instead of tapping him or her. Each runner can carry the same object, or a variety of objects.

Competition can be eliminated from the relay games by having the teams try to beat the clock. For instance, a team can go through a relay to establish a performance time, and then they repeat the relay to see if they can achieve a better time. In this way they are trying to do better as a group than in their previous trials. If two or more teams are playing, all the time scores are added together for a grand total, and this is the time to be beaten in subsequent collective efforts.

Relay races are exciting, raucous, and potentially silly events. One way to heighten the fun is to have the runner wear oversized adult clothes such as a hat, a scarf, a vest, or a pair of flippers. The hand-off involves removing the funny clothing, which must then be donned by the succeeding runner. Another interesting variation is one in which each child carries an empty tote bag; the runner's bag is filled with common objects, and in this case the hand-off involves removing the objects from one bag and filling the next one. True silliness is achieved in a similar variation when the hand-off involves a totally impractical number of objects carried in the runner's arms; there is great fumbling and dropping of objects in the process of running and handing them off.

Obstacle Course

Purpose

A sense of accomplishment and self-esteem are promoted through mastery of an obstacle course. A playground is a common expression of an obstacle course; it is typically great fun and very motivating. Whether temporarily set up by an adult or part of an established playground, an obstacle course fosters spatial awareness, motor planning, and coordination. This activity includes both motor and sensory challenges and places high demands on the child's ability to self-regulate. If the children set up the course, this activity also facilitates prosocial skills and social decision-making.

Description

The design possibilities of an obstacle course are endless, limited only by one's space, resources and imagination. An indoor obstacle course created by the practitioner should have four to six stations and provide a variety of experiences including sensory exploration, such as climbing over a hard object and then landing on a soft surface like an oversized floor pillow; moving through space, such as going under, around, and through objects; motor schemes, such as walking, jumping, crawling, climbing, and rolling; and use of other objects, such as scooter boards, barrels, and cardboard boxes.

Some of the most effective stations are simply designed, like using a sheet thrown over a mound of pillows to roll across or placing a yardstick between two chairs to step over or wiggle under.

An obstacle course has a starting and end point with a trail of stations in between. The adult can demonstrate how to negotiate the course and provide verbal directions; more typically, however, the children are encouraged to explore the course in their own idiosyncratic ways. One child proceeds into the course with the second child commencing when the first child is about halfway through; this pacing helps to limit the waiting time. Group motivation can be heightened by timing the collective performance to establish a baseline, with subsequent trials by the group aimed at beating the clock. This flexible activity can be used with children from ages 3–12.

Environment/Materials

Obstacle courses may be made outdoors on playgrounds or indoors in school gyms, therapy clinics, or classrooms. Equipment needs to be sturdy and safe. The hustle and bustle of this activity often generates a noisy environment.

Modifications

A challenge course may be created indoors, or, for older children, outdoors. For example, a course in a gymnasium may involve negotiating equipment arranged and sequenced in novel ways. Equipment can include parallel bars, ramps, rings, hanging ropes, and scooter boards. The children decide the order in which they will take turns on the equipment and who will be spotters for safety. The task can be made more demanding and fun by modifying requirements, like carrying a bucket of water or a backpack that is handed off to the person on the next piece of equipment. Children interpret a challenge course as very appealing and athletic because it is associated with nature centers, fitness programs, the Marines, and scouts.

Children who are younger or less motorically capable can be joined with an older peer to complete the course (peer mentoring). The first task is to coach the younger child who is negotiating the course, so the child is actively involved and rehearsing how to do the task. In this way the younger child has an opportunity for a social and motor experience. Another modification is to have a child go through the course backwards or blind-folded, increasing the developmental demands.

■ Art Activities

Wallpaper

Purpose

This activity creates a shared product through engagement in an associative play activity and is one way of progressing young children toward cooperative play.

Description

Create the wallpaper by decorating single sheets of paper in repeated patterns, so that each sheet is a replica of the others. A row of single sheets of drawing paper is placed on a table or the floor. Each child decides on a design that he or she would like to draw on the sheets, takes a crayon and draws the identical motif on each sheet. The children are in a row and progress systematically from one sheet to the next coloring their design. As the motifs are added, each paper is filled with designs and colors, and every sheet looks like the others. When they are as filled as the group members want them to be, the sheets are taped together as wallpaper and hung. The wallpaper becomes the identifying decoration for the group space and can be displayed each time the group meets. There should also be enough sheets to have one for each child to keep and take home. This activity is useful for younger children and for individuals with minimal skills.

Environment/Materials

Adequate space on a table or the floor is needed to allow a sufficient number of sheets of paper to be lined up in a row; the children need to be able to move freely around the paper layout.

Modifications

The activity can be simplified by having the children use stickers or ink stamps instead of drawing; this modification would be particularly helpful for children with poor fine motor control. The task can also be graded down by dividing the sheets into quadrants as a way of structuring the activity for children with poor visual spatial perception. If children have difficulty determining designs to draw, motifs can be suggested or assigned.

Collages

Purpose

The making of collages meets numerous therapeutic goals, and addresses all five components of social competence. Social and play behavior can be graded from parallel to cooperative levels of group interaction, and prosocial skills are highlighted through such behaviors as turn taking, sharing, and helping. Self-regulation is practiced through impulse control, monitoring distractibility, controlling tempers, and compromising. Communication involves active listening and conveying ideas, and social decision making is used in determining what to make and how to execute the task. Depending upon how the collage activity is designed, the intervention goals will shift among these five categories.

Description

A collage is a piece of artwork that uses paper, yarn, strips of cloth, and other materials to create a two-dimensional finished product. A simple form of collage can be made by a group of children who cut out magazine pictures and paste them on cardboard or poster board. Typically, the children are asked to use pictures that reflect information about each group member, such as group members' pets, favorite sports and foods, family members, and school events. The children search magazines for images that reflect this information, and the cut-out pictures are then pasted onto the board in a design agreed upon by the group. Some groups hang the finished collage in the room where they meet, while others choose to rotate owner-ship by having each group member take the collage home for a week. The collage is a highly versatile ther-apeutic medium that can be used with children from preschool to adolescence.

Environment/Materials

A horizontal work surface is most conducive to construction of a collage, and an adequate place is needed to store it while it dries; afterward, the collage can be hung vertically for display. Heavy stock paper is best because paper products like newspaper are too thin and do not work well with glue. Water-based glues should be used sparingly because they pucker the paper. Many magazines have inappropriate images for children; for this reason it is often best to pre-select pictures from magazines and categorize them in folders. Keep in mind the cultural sensitivity of family members in the selection of magazines and pictures.

Modifications

Create a simple **triptych** by dividing a long piece of cardboard or paper into three sections and choosing a theme for decorating. When working with children at age 5, each section can be labeled as a room from home, such as the kitchen, living room, and bedroom. The children can look through catalogs or newspaper advertising supplements to find furniture and room decorations appropriate to each of the three rooms. They cut out the pictures and paste them on the triptych creating their ideal rooms. A similar triptych can be made with the theme of a zoo. The collage is divided into three sections of mountains, plains, and rivers. The children paint the appropriate background motif and then cut out or draw animals and objects that relate to each environmental setting. Encourage the children's imagination by incorporating found objects such as twigs, shells and pennies into the collage. Yet another theme that can be used for a triptych is vacations in varied locales, such as the city, the mountains, or the beach.

Create a **face collage** by having the children cut out faces that express different emotions. Emphasize social perception by having the pictures depict young and old individuals of both sexes; the children have to discern and label each facial expression properly, and a list of moods and emotions shown on the faces is placed in a prominent place on the collage. This list is generated after the collage is created and the children have an opportunity to stand back and reflect on the faces they have used. The face collage can be used effectively with children age 8 and older.

Construct a **group book** out of a large piece of cardboard that is about three by five feet in size and divide it in the middle so that it can be opened and closed like a book. The children cut out magazine pictures of objects that depict the interests and preferences of other people in the group and place them in a pile; this is a shift from collecting for oneself to focusing on others. The children sort the collected pictures following the rule of offering appropriate pictures to peers as they find them; in this manner, everyone accumulates personalized pictures without asking for or taking them. It is important for the practitioner to model this process, verbally announcing finds enthusiastically, such as, "Oh, Mike! Here is a picture of a Game Boy, just like yours!" Each child gets an assortment of representative pictures and pastes them on the inside of the book in a section marked with his or her name. There is great power in pictures that represent meaningful aspects of the child's life and personality. The pictures need to be appealing and cool so the children will be highly motivated to acquire them for their section of the book by adhering to the rules in order to earn pictures from others.

Have a small groups of children (about three to four in a group) assemble a **puzzle collage**. Each group secretly identifies someone from a different group as the subject of the collage. The collage is made on poster board or on lightweight cardboard, and selected pictures from newspapers or magazines are glued on the board. Once assembled, the collages are cut into large pieces in the style of a jigsaw puzzle. This can be done simply; cardboard can be cut on straight lines while poster board is easiest to cut along curvilinear lines. The groups then give the unassembled puzzle to peers in another group to put together. The final task is for each group to figure out who is the mystery person on each collage. Secrecy is the exciting element in this task and motivates the children. The puzzle collage is most appropriate for children age 8 and older.

The **body collage** is a group effort in which all the children make a large human figure comprised of body parts cut out of magazines. The task starts with the practitioner drawing a large outline of the body, at least 4 or 5 feet tall. The children cut out as many body parts as they can find so that there are multiple arms, legs, feet, hands, and the like. When numerous pictures of body parts have been collected, the group members glue them on the large figure in the appropriate location until the figure is completely filled in with pictures. When the gluing is completed, each section of the body is composed of smaller images of that body part, so that the arm has many arms glued to it and the hand is composed of multiple hands, etc. The result is a modern art cubist effect. The face is an exception; it can be made of multiple magazine faces but the features need to be drawn in so that the face has a normal appearance.

Life-Sized Portraits

Purpose

This activity helps a child learn and practice the roles of leader and follower. The child learns to de-center from his or her narcissistic perspective, becoming accustomed to being in charge at some times and following at others. Prosocial behaviors are emphasized throughout the activity.

Description

The children work in pairs to create a life-sized portrait of each other. The partners take turns lying down on large sheets of paper in order to draw the outline of their bodies. The children can decide the pose that they wish to have outlined, such as flying like a super hero or making a jump shot. The portraits are completed by coloring, painting, or gluing fabric, paper, or other materials. The child whose portrait is being completed (the "boss") determines the job assignments. These assignments have to do with how the interior of the portrait will look; in the space around the portrait the children are encouraged to depict favorite objects, interests, and experiences of the individual. The boss has the final say on what and how things will be done. However, the partner (the "helper") is encouraged to offer ideas. Both children are coached to communicate in a prosocial manner so that their ideas will be embraced rather than rejected. After one portrait is completed, the children switch roles and complete the other one.

A nice finale to this activity is to have all the life-sized portraits hung around the room and a special showing held for parents, school personnel, or other children. Each pair of children introduces their partners and the artwork, describing how the portrait was made and all they have come to know about their partner. The children get to keep the artwork that they produced.

Environment/Materials

This activity has substantial space requirements. The sheets of paper need to be at least 5 feet by 3 feet for each full-size portrait. In addition, two children must work on them on the floor or on a table with plenty of room to move around the paper. The paper can be a large single sheet or smaller pieces taped together. Any medium can be used to color the portraits such as markers, crayons, pastels, paint or a combination. These portraits usually require more than one session to complete, so adequate storage space is needed to keep them safe.

Modifications

Some children have difficulty in ideation and motor planning. They have difficulty formulating the goal for action and problem solving the sequential steps for accomplishing the plan. They cannot organize themselves in terms of knowing what to do, how to start, and where to go next. Therefore, these children need a lot of structure and guidance in the role of the boss. The adult can pose simple choice questions to help the child focus, along the lines of "Do you want to begin with the legs or the arms?" and then gently guide the child through the overall task. For the child who is overwhelmed with the larger spaces, the figure can be divided into smaller sections that can be worked on in turn. In this way boundaries are clear, and space is manageable.

Musical Activities

Purpose

Musical activities are excellent for children of all ages for numerous reasons. They are highly motivating, invite participation, and are familiar. They foster playfulness and a sense of joy; they also create a bond among the children for group cohesion. Musical activities run the gamut of arousal levels from calming to exciting. Most are easily repeated, and repetition allows all the children to acquire the desired skills. When accompanied by action, music organizes children's motor skills; and music often fosters language skills in children with communication disorders.

Description

A common folk song that is highly appealing to children because of its playful qualities is "I Know an Old Lady Who Swallowed a Fly." With each verse, the song becomes more absurd as the old lady swallows a spider, bird, cat, dog, goat, cow, and horse. The cadence tends to build with the children becoming increasingly more excited and silly. For young children, or those with developmental delays, a visual display to guide them through the verses is helpful. Depending upon their artistic skills, children can draw or color each part of the song on a separate piece of paper, making a picture of the old lady, the spider, the bird, and so on. The pictures can be displayed on a wall in the sequence of the song, and group members can take turns acting as the leader by pointing to the pictures to indicate the verse to be sung.

Environment/Materials

This activity can be done in any space where there is enough room for drawing the pictures. Materials needed include paper, crayons or markers, and tape to hang the pictures on the wall.

Modifications

Another example that lends itself to this format is "On Top of Spaghetti," a takeoff on the song "On Top of Old Smokey." Of course, action songs are commonly sung and commercially available through songbooks and tapes; these combine the musical rhythm of the song with expressive physical gestures. Examples include "The Hokey Pokey," "The Itsy Bitsy Spider," "If You're Happy and You Know It," and "She'll Be Comin' Round the Mountain." Part of the success of an action song depends on the ability of the adult to exaggerate and extend the song and its gestures.

Puppetry

Purpose

The goals of puppetry are communication and collaboration. Mutual decision-making is involved when two children are making one puppet and must determine who the puppet will be and what it will look like. Rich dialogue emerges from puppet construction and later story telling.

Description

Puppetry is imaginary play with pretend characters and can be conducted using stuffed toys, dolls, or puppets that are commercially available or homemade. Hand puppets can be simple to construct. Two pieces of felt or fabric are cut out in sizes and shapes that fit the front and back of the child's hand. A third piece, in the shape of an oval, creates the puppet's mouth. The oval piece is folded in half and attached to the top and bottom of the puppet. Lining the mouth with cardboard from a file folder to provide stability may be helpful. The remainder of the arm is also attached, with all attachments made by gluing or sewing the pieces together. The facial features of the puppet can be drawn using a fabric marker. Special characteristics, such as eyes or hair, can be created using yarn and buttons or other found objects.

Puppet play can occur in two basic forms. The children can set a scene and spontaneously play with the puppets in an informal manner. Older children may prefer to write a story and have a script to read; this is particularly helpful with less verbal children. Puppetry is appropriate for children age 3–12.

Environment/Materials

Puppetry can be conducted in a small space. If the puppetry becomes more elaborate, a "stage" space may be necessary. The stage can be improvised from a piece of furniture, formed by a large sheet suspended across the room, constructed from cardboard boxes, or purchased commercially.

Modifications

When used without props, puppetry can be simple and involve spontaneous play. A more complex approach would include the construction of a stage with background scenery that changes with each act of the story line. The presentation can be conducted for a live audience of children and family members or can be videotaped for later showing. The use of stuffed toys is particularly helpful for children with motor deficits by eliminating the need for fine manipulation of puppet mouthpieces. For children who have difficulty memorizing their lines or reading normal print, the script can be written on poster board in large letters and propped up at the side of the puppeteer for easy reading.

Construction Activities

Wooden Sculpture

Purpose

The primary goal of this activity is to develop a level of comfort and attachment to the group. A secondary goal is the planning and execution of an unstructured construction activity.

Description

Each child in the group assembles a construction made out of wood and other found objects. For instance, the child may construct a crude boat, a car, a sailfish, or a free-form object using varied items such as washers, nuts, bolts, wire, or screws. The constructions are then assembled into one final product that includes a message related to the group, such as "Group in Session" or "Carpenters at Work" or "Woodwork is Fun." In this manner, parallel play and associative play are the primary social modes of the activity, but themes of cooperative play are introduced by having a common end product. The wooden sculpture activity is best used for children with fair to good motor coordination and an adequate attention span and is best suited for children age ten or older.

Because this activity takes 2 or more weeks to reach its conclusion, the group process will evolve over time. The processing issues include developing a sense of the physical environment in the "workshop," negotiating turns and sharing tools, becoming aware of the roles of the participants in the room, and, learning the tone of the group (e.g., informal, fun, respectful, and supportive). In beginning a new group, having a unifying activity that is fun and builds cohesion is important. The wooden sculpture activity is excellent for this purpose. The level of interaction increases as the sculpture progresses from individual pieces to one larger whole.

Environment/Materials

The space needs to accommodate a table large enough for all participants to work comfortably, and the work surface should be protected from harm. Needed materials and equipment include woodworking tools, wood scraps, and other items commonly used in construction tasks. This type of activity is very noisy.

Modifications

You can simplify the task by giving a specific job and materials to each child; this is particularly helpful for children who are disorganized or new to the medium. The complexity can be increased by having the children work with a partner to design part of the sculpture or by requiring each child to use all the tools and materials that are available. Another modification is to use paper products, tape, and wire for the sculpture instead of wood; creative constructions can be made from cardboard, paper, fabric, and found objects such as buttons, paper clips, twigs, scraps of fabric, and string.

Building With Blocks

Purpose

Building with blocks is a flexible activity that can be used appropriately with children from pre-school to age eleven. Block building with a partner or in a small group is an excellent activity for decreasing egocentricity and fostering the ability to take the perspective of others. It expands the play repertoire of children and promotes constructive and dramatic play. Imagination is strengthened during the development of, and the subsequent play with, the constructions.

This activity provides an opportunity to learn and practice prosocial skills such as asking, giving, and negotiating. Social decision making is involved in the planning and implementation of the play. Building with blocks is particularly effective for children who have language deficits but strengths in the arenas of visual spatial skills and nonverbal communication. These children shine in block construction, which enhances their prestige in the group and their self-esteem.

Description

A standard format for block building is to have children on the floor in pairs or small groups. Children grouped together must agree on one structure to make; efforts cannot be divided, and a basic rule is that no child can undo the work of another child. Children in the age 5–8 range typically make structures such as castles, forts, science fiction sets, and towns. Any prop from the environment may be used to supplement the blocks; these may include toy cars for the roadway and found objects for streetlights. Providing blocks in varied sizes, shapes, and colors will facilitate the creativity of the children.

Environment/Materials

Floor space must be able to accommodate the movement and sprawl of children actively engaged in construction activities. Also, the more varied the blocks are in shape and size, the better.

Modifications

The following two modifications are appropriate for children who are young, impulsive, and egocentric, as they often have few ideas and limited creativity. Because ideation is poor, such children cannot visualize a product to build. They require maximal structure and adaptation to engage successfully in block building. In the first modification, visual boundaries can be established by placing a sheet of cardboard on the floor. For some children, this is all that is necessary to give them a starting point for building; other children can edge the boundary of the cardboard with blocks in order to make a wall. With this structure they can create walls with windows and other embellishments. In the second modification, two teams are given identically matched sets of blocks. The goal of this activity is to use all of the blocks for a single construction. Each team takes a turn putting a block out, and the other team matches it with an identical block, that is, positioning it on the floor in the same way as the original block. Then they reverse roles being the builder and the copier as the second team adds a new block to the emerging structure and the other team responds in exactly the same manner. When the blocks are used up, the structure is complete.

While some children do not have an idea of what to construct, other children have difficulties in prosocial skills and social perspective taking; they are often quite bright but very egocentric. Although potentially desirable play partners related to their creativity, these children are often shunned because of their narcissism and insistence on having things done their way. Because they are oblivious to the ideas and needs of their peers, such children come across as selfish and controlling and as a result are either rejected or ignored by peers. The following two forms of block building are specifically designed to help them function in a more collaborative manner.

In the first variation, each team decides on one structure and goes to a pretend "store" to attain building supplies. The initial construction plan must be specific because the blocks are distributed to accommodate that plan, and a team can only "purchase" a set number of blocks with each visit to the store. If other teams deplete the store's supply of a desired block, the team must adapt and revise their plan. The constructions are considered complete after a designated time period. During this activity team members have had the opportunity to work together to decide the structure to be built, plan the design of the construction, determine the required materials, and build the structure. This repetitive process allows each child to practice new skills related to social perspective taking and to use prosocial behaviors. Numerous sessions can be dedicated to this activity to ensure that the new behaviors become automatic.

A second modification in which block building can be also graded up for children with good construction skills and creativity but problems with egocentricity is to provide materials that are novel and complex. These materials may include construction toys such as Ramagon®, K'nex®, and Tinker Toys®, combining Legos® with blocks or commercially available marble mazes. The children's motivation to participate is strong because they are eager to experiment with these enticing materials. The requirement to make only one structure forces them to use the materials collaboratively. Within one social competence group there is likely to be multiple levels of construction skill. With proper therapeutic structure, even the children with the least abilities can create a structure that is admirable. As children's skills expand, professional demands can increase. For example, Group A should build a structure as tall as possible; Group B should construct a structure as long as possible; and Group C should create a structure with multiple openings.

Numerous variations exist in building with blocks; other modifications include having the children follow a three-dimensional model, a pictorial diagram, or written directions.

Floor Puzzles

Purpose

This activity has several benefits for improved social and play behavior. Floor puzzles foster teamwork and cooperative play when they are executed by groups of children. They also enhance social perspective taking and decrease egocentricity. Through problem solving together, the children practice shared decision-making. This activity also enables many children who have language difficulties to excel and shine in a social activity. Their skills in visual-spatial tasks usually do not help them in the social encounters that require language. Puzzles provide a unique opportunity to demonstrate skills in the context of social play.

Description

A wide variety of commercially available floor puzzles are appropriate for all age ranges. The complexity is based on the number of puzzle pieces required as well as the intricacy of the design. Themes include such topics as currently popular characters such as The Rugrats™ or Spider-Man®, educational content such as the ABCs and nature. Two or more players work together to assemble the pieces. The social exchanges include sharing pieces, asking for help, problem solving, and celebrating success.

Environment/Materials

The puzzle pieces come in many sizes and shapes. Experience suggests that a 16-inch width is the minimum desirable size, with a 3- to 4-foot total dimension preferable for group interaction. Puzzles with 14 to 30 pieces work best and the box cover photo is used as a guide. A large sheet of cardboard can be placed on the floor to demarcate the space for assembling the puzzle if desired. Typically, the children huddle and sprawl around the puzzle on the floor. The activity has been used successfully with children up to age 14.

Modifications

An interesting innovation is to have the group divided into two or more teams. Each team assembles a floor puzzle that is appropriate to its developmental level. The teams can compete with each other for who is the fastest to complete a puzzle, or each team can work separately trying to improve its fastest time.

Another modification is to give roles to different individuals in the group. The "supplier" distributes the puzzle pieces to the "player" who assembles them; the player can request pieces of a certain shape or color from the supplier. Roles are rotated after a specified number of pieces are in place. There is give and take between participants regarding how to construct the puzzle, and this modification increases the verbal and interactive component of play.

Sometimes the floor puzzle can be embedded into another larger activity. An obstacle course can be designed that has puzzle pieces distributed throughout the course or at the end of the course; in either case, the children pick up one or more pieces and assemble the puzzle at the end of the course. This activity fosters a sense of camaraderie and increased interest in completing the puzzle.

Games

Ball Play

Purpose

Ball play activities range widely from simple, informal games to complex team activities, thus the goals of ball play are variable based on the way the game is structured. Ball activities can be adapted to address numerous outcomes. Self-regulation is highlighted as the children monitor their energy levels and learn to stay on task; prosocial skills are emphasized such as following rules, cheering peers on, and turn taking; gross and fine motor skills are learned and practiced; cooperative play and awareness of others are fostered. Four types of ball play are described—passing games, modified volleyball, target games, and standard team sports.

Passing Games

Description

The children sit in a circle. One child has the ball and states a fact of personal information about another child as he or she rolls it to that child. Examples include, "I am going to roll the ball to a person who is wearing sneakers" or "I am going to roll the ball to a person who has a sister named Sally." The game continues as the children have multiple turns passing. This activity is useful for developing group cohesion; the children must hear and remember facts about their peers and maintain observation of the total group. This is a good warm-up for a variety of ages: a group of preschool children can use a 24-inch therapy ball, while adolescents can use a 17-pound medicine ball.

Environment/Materials

Passing games can be readily played indoors or outdoors as long as there is ample space for the group. Balls can be varied in size, shape, texture, and weight.

Modification

A variation of this game involves passing balls of different sizes and weight. The children can be in a circle or in opposing lines, and the ball, beanbag, or other object can be passed in different directions to the next person, the person across, or to any one randomly. The children can also be standing, kneeling, or sitting on an unsteady support such as a T-stool. If the children are in a standing position, the ball can be passed overhead, between the legs, with one or two hands, or in other ways decided by group members to add interest and motor demands.

Modified Volleyball

Description

A string, rope, or net can be stretched across an open space. The children, divided into two teams, play volleyball using the standard rules. Especially for use indoors, the ball can be a balloon, beanbag, Nerf® ball, Koosh® ball, or balls of varied texture. Three options are available for scoring. The teams can play against each other in competitive fashion; a collective score can be determined, such as, the total number of passes between the teams; or a collective time can be derived, such as the total time the ball is in the air not touching the floor for the combined teams. Collective scoring eliminates having winners and losers.

Environment/Materials

Modified volleyball allows a vigorous gross motor activity to be conducted indoors. Due to the excitement of the game, the children are typically noisy.

Modification

Modified volleyball can be played sitting, standing, or kneeling. In addition, the rules can be altered so that the children catch the ball instead of it tapping back, or pass the ball to a teammate who returns it to the opposing team. Complexity can also be introduced by having more than one ball in play.

Target Games

Description

Shooting baskets on the playground is a common, age-appropriate leisure time activity. The children gain skills that are readily transferable to their everyday activities.

Environment/Materials

Variations of target games can be played indoors or outdoors depending on available resources.

Modification

The children can throw balls of varying sizes and textures at a target such as a trashcan or beanbag target. They can also ride on hanging equipment and toss the ball at a defined target. Another modification is to play basketball while propelling oneself on a scooter board. The group members can decide how the game will be played.

Standard Team Sports

Description

Ball play can be conducted in a way that helps children develop social comfort in team sports as they acquire physical skills. Routine games such as baseball, basketball, soccer, and dodge ball are familiar and appropriate for peer play. Some children with social problems do not enjoy group sports; their lack of interest is often related to a history of social stigma in team activities. They may be self-conscious, have a fear of failure, or feel socially incompetent. Other children may have poor motor skills that undermine competitive participation, and may have experienced "the last to be chosen and first to be out" syndrome.

Ball play in a social competence group provides a rare opportunity for these children to be able to play group sports in an environment that is supportive and accentuates their strengths.

Environment/Materials

In general, an outdoor playing field and gymnasium are optimal for team sports.

Modification

There is a validated approach to teaching children ball playing skills that practically assures success. Children learn to hit, throw, or catch because anxiety is decreased and motivation is increased. The key is to pick the element of the team sport that is most captivating and work on increasing that particular skill by making a game of that skill alone. For example, the most attractive aspect of basketball is shooting a basket to get a point, whereas for baseball the major attraction is hitting the ball and getting on base. Modifications may be required with the equipment; one can make a basketball hoop out of a cardboard box that has a hole cut in it and which has been attached to a rope or pole so the height can be adjusted for each player. This alteration is appropriate for young and hesitant learners. A Nerf ball and a Wiffle® ball bat may be used for young children or beginners in baseball.

Another baseball modification is to use real bats but change the ball. An 8-inch rubber ball can be used to start, and play can progress to a softball size. This way the child has ample practice swinging the bat and indeed plays until he or she hits the ball, as players ignore the rule that three strikes constitute an out and the end of a turn. Any hitting of the ball counts, and when the child gets a hit he or she runs the bases. The children decide as the game progresses when to move to a smaller ball. As mastery develops, more standard game rules are introduced.

Scavenger Hunt

Purpose

A scavenger hunt is excellent for team building, as it involves problem solving, communication, and self-regulation among team members. Because this activity is frequently played at birthday parties, developing skills in scavenger hunting enhances the child's play repertoire.

Description

This activity involves locating found objects in the environment. The children are divided into one or more teams and given a list of objects to be found. The objects are not necessarily hidden in the environment but can be identified by searching and include common objects such as a paper clip, shoelaces, three round stones, and a 5-inch twig. The hunt is started when the practitioner says, "You have 10 minutes to find up to 15 objects." If two or more teams are playing, they can have the same or different lists of objects to be discovered. The game ends when the time is up, and the children count how many objects they correctly acquired.

Environment

A scavenger hunt can be played indoors but is often more exciting when conducted outside.

Modifications

The list of objects can be replaced by providing clues that indicate what must be found. For instance, instead of listing "a magnolia leaf," the clues could state that it is large, grows on a tree with white flowers, and has a deep green color. The clues need to be written so that the participants will struggle to figure out the answer but can succeed with effort.

A variation of a scavenger hunt can be designed to fit well into a classroom environment. The children are divided into two or more teams, and a list of clues is provided to each team that requires problem solving, calculation, and interaction. The following are sample clues that can be written for the children.

- Estimate how many pencils can be laid end to end from the chalkboard to the closet in our room. Write it down and check it out.

- Estimate how many body lengths of members of the class there are from the front door of the school to the door of your classroom. Write it down and check it out.

- Estimate how many table legs are in your classroom. Write it down and check it out.

- Make a list of the teachers and assistants in your grade.

- Draw a map of your school and indicate where each class is.

- Draw a map of the climbing equipment on the playground. Include everything you remember. Provide details so that the map is clearly understood.

A treasure hunt can also be played. One or more teams must find a "treasure" by following a series of hidden clues. The first clue is given to the children; from there they must search for the second clue, which provides the necessary information for locating the third clue, and this sequence is continued until the final clue leads to the secret treasure. Generally the treasure hunt is less frenzied and more interactive than the scavenger hunt. Self-regulation is practiced as the participants suppress the drive to use clues out of order or read clues belonging to other teams.

Life-Sized Monopoly®

Purpose

Playing life-sized Monopoly® facilitates such prosocial skills as following rules, taking turns, answering questions, asking for help, and accepting compliments. Learning to attend to multiple issues at one time enhances self-regulation, management of excitement and frustration, dealing with competition, and fosters communication skills in the process of trading and negotiating. Because the game involves having a silent partner, nonverbal communication is practiced.

Description

The standard Monopoly board is made into an oversized reproduction by using one white king-size flat sheet. The sheet is cut into panels for each side of the board, and squares are cut for each corner. Each property is drawn on the sheet large enough for two kids to stand on the property, and the children can color the properties with fabric marker. The person who plays the banker can sit in the middle of the board. The Chance, Community Chest, and property cards are used from the standard board game, as is the play money from the game. Oversized dice can add to the fun, and children's colored building blocks can be used to represent houses and hotels. Children from age 8 to 80 enjoy this game.

Basic rules stay the same as in the standard Monopoly board game. However, additional rules are introduced to facilitate attainment of the goals. Children play with partners or small teams, and each member of the team takes a turn being the board "piece;" whenever the team passes GO, the players change places. The player on the board may not speak; and all decisions about purchasing or trading must reflect the opinions of all team members, including the silent partner. If the silent partner speaks, the team loses a turn.

Environment/Materials

A large space is required to play life-sized Monopoly. The game is noisy because there is active discussion among team members and the banker.

Modifications

Because it takes hours to play to conclusion, the game continues week after week in a social competence group. The children must lay the board out at the start of play and pack it up at the end of each session; each team can have a chart to track ownership of properties and an envelope to hold its money.

Note: An abbreviated version of life-sized Monopoly is an excellent game for special events when mixed ages, including adults, are present.

■ Verbal Activities

Interviewing

Purpose

The primary goal of the interviewing activity is to enhance communication by learning to pose questions, attend to and remember information, and share the information in a conversational style. In this way the child develops the ability to take the perspective of another child and learns how to introduce a child into a group. A secondary goal is to foster attachment to the group. Interviewing facilitates group cohesion and helps a new child join the group. Because it provides a personal welcome, an interview lessens resistance to the group.

Description

The children generate a list of questions that could be asked of someone that they just met. Sample questions include:

- Do you have a pet?

- Do you like sports?

- What is your favorite food?

- Do you have any brothers or sisters?

- What is your favorite TV show?

The children are then divided into pairs and asked to interview their partner. The interviewer asks three questions from the list and must remember the answers. Later, the interviewer reports back to the larger group about what he or she discovered about the partner. Each child begins the report by introducing the person: "This is Gordon. He . . ."

Interviewing as a therapeutic activity is appropriate for all types of children and levels of skill. This activity requires close guidance by an adult to assure that the participants remain on track, that is, to prevent the children from being tangential or one child from taking over.

Environment/Materials

The questions can be written on a large piece of paper and posted where all group members can observe them. Pairs of children should be physically spaced out during the interview process so that each set of partners can focus on each other.

Modifications

A number of modifications can be made for children who have language difficulties. A list of questions can be left in an easily visible location so that they can be referred to at any time by the children; icons or pictures can be used to represent questions for children who cannot read. The interviewer can write down responses to questions if auditory memory is a problem.

To foster creative thinking, the interviewee can pretend to be a character such as a rock star or astronaut. In this way the interview process is less threatening and personal. This modification is particularly helpful for children who tend to depend on "scripts" or stylized, superficial, and inflexible use of language.

There are three ways to grade the complexity of the interview process. First, the interviewer can be expected to ask three questions from the list as previously described. Second, the interviewer can choose a topic from the list and make up three relevant questions. Third, the interviewer can pick a topic and ask a related question, and based upon the interviewee's answer, a new question can be formulated. This last option approximates the natural progression seen in conversation, and the partners automatically begin to interject comments into the interview and forget the presence of the adult; without realizing it, they engage in conversation. After any of these interview formats, the interviewer reports back to the group.

Bop It

Purpose

The Bop It game requires the player to manage his or her level of excitement while listening to a command of the toy; then the player must rapidly respond by handing the toy to the next person, who in turn will follow the next direction. The purposes of this activity are to foster listening skills while in an excited state and to be able to organize a speedy physical response. Social-emotional interaction is a major outcome of this experience.

Description

Bop It is a battery-powered toy with voice commands. Made of colorful plastic, this narrow toy is about 18 inches long. There is a button in its middle to "bop," a knob at one end to pull, and a knob at the other end to twist. The voice randomly commands three different actions: "Bop It," "pull it," and "twist it." The corresponding action is to follow the command that must be performed within a few seconds of the command. If accomplished in time, another command is automatically given; if the correct action is not taken in time, the toy makes a crashing sound to signal the end of that round. The toy then beeps once for each successful response; for example, if four actions were done in a row before crashing, four beeps are played back immediately after the crash.

The activity can be played with two or more children to make it a social game. A standard method of operation is for each child to take a turn playing the game until he or she crashes, and the winner is the one who gets the most beeps. There is a shared version that includes a command to "pass it." This is a very exciting and fun-filled game in which the children tend to laugh when someone crashes. Bop It is appropriate for children ages 4–12.

Environment/Materials

The Bop It game is available from Parker Brothers. Floor space for about four sitting people is required. The practitioner must know how to program and operate the toy.

Modifications

One modification is to pass the toy after each action to other group members who are seated in a circle. For instance, a player bops it, pulls it, or twists it based on the command from the toy and then quickly hands it to the next player before the next command. In this variation on the game the focus is not competitive but instead on shared group success.

A more difficult modification is to assign different actions to different people. For example, one or more individuals bop it, pull it, or twist it. The toy is quickly handed off among the players based on the random commands. Each participant must be aware of the instruction from the toy as well as the role of each player. This version of the game requires very rapid processing of auditory input and the execution of a quick physical response to an appropriate individual. If desired, one can divide the group into teams with separate Bop It toys. The teams can play competitively with each other to see who scores the highest number of beeps or just try to better their own records.

Where's Waldo?

Purpose

The goal of this activity is to expand expressive language within an instrumental interaction.

Description

"Where's Waldo?" is a copyright of Martin Hanford. Posters are commercially available in assorted sizes and varying complexity. The practitioner chooses a poster at an appropriate level of challenge for the participating children in the group. The adult describes an item that is hidden in the poster that the children are to find, and they are encouraged to work together. The adult models expressive language related to directions and systematic strategies for the search, such as "look to the right," "you are near it," "you are getting cold," or "it's toward the top." The first child to find the item provides cues to the others until everyone has located the item. "Where's Waldo?" is suitable for children ages 6–9.

Environment/Materials

This game can be played on a tabletop or on the floor. The floor setting fosters informal lounging of the children for a relaxed time and promotes acceptance of close physical proximity with others.

Modifications

The game can be simplified in a number of ways. The poster can be taped into quadrants or columns to narrow the field for scanning and provide visual cues. One can also cover the poster except for one section with a piece of paper in order to narrow the field for searching. Another option for simplification is to cut a hole in cardboard and use it as a way of focusing the child's gaze; the child slides the cardboard systematically from side to side or top to bottom to structure the search.

The children can be divided into teams of two or three to foster socialization and language development, and one team gives directions for the other team to follow. Each team identifies what the other team will be looking for and determines how the item will be described. In this way one grades the complexity of the language processing. For example, a team could say "Find a man who is doing tricks over a horse," or "Find a man who is a gymnast over a horse," or "Find a man who is a gymnast with an animal."

Another modification requiring advanced language use is a form of 20 Questions. One team chooses an item but does not share it with the other team. The searching team must ask questions to direct and guide its exploration, and only questions that elicit a *yes* or *no* response may be used. Acceptable questions include, "Is it one person?" or "Is it at the top?" or "Are the men running?" This modification reinforces the language needed in instrumental interactions.

Because this activity is centered on a complex picture, plenty of opportunity is provided for the repetition of language, visual, and interactive skills, and one can search for item after item with sustained interest and motivation. There are many occasions for the adults to participate and model searching strategies. The children especially enjoy deciding on what they wish the adult to find, that is, "stumping the adult."

Quiz Show

Purpose

A major goal of this activity is to reduce egocentricity by having the children pay attention to each other and learn information about their peers. A communication goal is the ability to negotiate responses to answers, and self-regulation is addressed because the children are not allowed to blurt out answers.

Description

Adapt a large, game spinner, such as one from the Twister™ game, to show the names of the children playing. This is easily accomplished by covering the board with plain white paper with a slit in it from the center of one edge to the center of the paper, which makes it possible to slide the paper onto the board, covering it but allowing the spinner to work freely over the paper. Draw a circle on the paper and divide into 16 sections. The initials or names of each player are written in the segments. Other designations can be used to fill in unused spots as there will be extra places in the circle. These designations could be "spin again," "free choice," or something decided by the group members.

The children are divided into teams of two to four members. The adult starts the game by flicking the spinner on the game board. The spinner lands on a child's name and that team must share some information about the child; this information has been gathered through common experiences such as circle time, snack, or general group activity. Each individual team determines its own rules of operation, such as who will be the spokesperson and the spinner. After a team member provides the information, a flick of the spinner initiates the next turn and the next team repeats the process.

Environment/Materials

Space needs to be adequate so that the teams can work with privacy on their answers. The game is rather sedentary and can be played on the floor or at a table.

Modifications

One alteration is to use a spinning board from another type of game or to create one's own spinner. If this is not possible, dice can be used as a substitute; the names of the participants are given a number from one to twelve with extra numbers randomly assigned to "free choice," "throw again," or a designation determined by the group. The team can throw dice and the total dots on the dice yield the number for a child's name, and that name is then the target for the information to be shared.

One variation is that a team's spokesperson must give two or three pieces of information. This information must be in a category chosen by the team, such as favorite foods, summer vacation, preferred sport, family members, or pets. After a team has reported specific information about a child, the same information cannot be used in subsequent turns.

The heart of this task is the shared focus on information about each other in a game format. Two or more sessions may be required for the participants to learn all the rules for the game and be comfortable with them. A reward for winning could be the team choosing, from a list provided by the adult, which play activities will be scheduled for the next session.

This game is highly motivating because it gives the group members control over what will occur. It provides an opportunity for the group members to practice prosocial skills such as considering and offering activities that will be appealing to peers.

Who Am I?

Purpose

This activity fosters conversational skills, particularly asking questions in a contingent way.

Description

Each child has the name of another participant pinned to his or her back, and each tries to guess the name by walking around the room and, assuming the unknown identity, asking first person questions of others about notable characteristics that might provide clues. "Am I tall?" and "Do I like sports?" and "Do I collect baseball caps?" are acceptable questions, as the only answers allowed are "yes" and "no," and the only such question not allowed is "Am I" and the name of a child. The game is complete when each child indicates he or she knows the person whose name is on his or her back. Questioning stops and each person announces a name. This activity is appropriate for children ages 8–12.

Environment/Materials

The space needs to be sufficient to allow the children to move freely around the room asking questions. Because this is essentially a language game, there is little need for materials other than name cards, markers, and pins.

Modifications

Without changing the manner of playing the game, the themes of what is placed on everyone's back can be altered. Themes can focus on emotions, famous people, or jobs.

Another variation of "Who am I?" involves having the children write three clues about themselves on a card; sample responses include "I like to read comic books," "I have a flat top," and "I have two brothers." The cards are placed in a bag or box; each child pulls out a card and guesses to whom it belongs. If the guess is incorrect, all the children in the group can freely make a guess. If one pulls out one's own card, it is returned to the bag after another card has been chosen. The game is completed when all the cards have been chosen and all the children identified. This activity is excellent in the orientation phase of getting to know members of a new group.

Video Role-playing

Purpose

In this activity the children are able to talk about their social problems, experiences, and emotions, and together they explore solutions to the problems raised. The children practice prosocial skills for dealing with these issues through role-playing.

Description

The children develop scripts that they later role-play in front of the video camera. These scripts typically address issues of concern that they have regarding unpleasant social experiences. Sample scripts may focus on being teased, resolving conflict, introducing oneself to a group, managing embarrassing circumstances, and dealing with the cafeteria, bus stop, and the locker room. Typically, the adult needs to help the children generate ideas, develop scripts or scenarios around each idea, and sequence these into a narrative. This is a high-level and demanding task that is appropriate for children from age 9 who are cognitively able. Because it is emotionally laden, some children may be uncomfortable having their role-play videotaped. For these children, the videotape scripts can be acted by puppets or stuffed animals or represented by a sequence of illustrations with a voice over to tell the story.

Each group of children will decide for themselves how best to do the actual shooting of the videotape. Some groups will be quite concrete and assign roles to different participants, such as director, cameraman, and scriptwriter. Other groups will choose to share the tasks and work in a more collaborative framework. The practitioner assumes a variety of roles as needed, including teacher, facilitator, resource person, or coach; determination of the role is based upon the changing needs of the children and the nature of the group process.

Environment/Materials

As a prelude to doing this activity, children should practice using the video camera; that is, filming, zooming in for close-ups, fading, and following the action. Printed instructions on how to use the camera are helpful. More than one tape is needed if each child is to have a tape to take home; an alternative is to have a showing of the completed video for parents or friends. Some children are motivated to produce the video as a tool for educating adults about their social experiences in order to help other children.

Modifications

The video role-play can be directed toward creative fun instead of serious social problem solving. The children may like to tape gross motor activities, conversation during snack time, recess and hanging out together, or completion of a board game. Therefore the children share playful life experiences that foster attachment to group members.

Imaginary Play Activities

Mime Phrases

Purpose

The major purpose of this activity is to increase social perception through reading and conveying nonverbal cues and body language.

Description

This game is a variant on charades. The children are divided into two teams, and each team draws a card that has a phrase printed on it. The phrases describe everyday events or activities, familiar stories and cartoon characters, or something comical. In turn, each player on the team pantomimes the phrase that is on the card, and team members try to guess the phrase in a certain amount of time. The game is played until everyone has had a turn. Each team gets a point for a correct guess, and the team with the most points is the winner.

The theatrical nature of the phrases is critical to the enjoyment and success of the game. The more playful the game, the harder the children will work at this difficult task of nonverbal communication. The following phrases have been used effectively in social competence groups.

Swimming under water	Dentist pulling a tooth
Riding a horse	Frog catching a fly
Raising a flag up a pole	Dog burying a bone
Eating an apple	Buttering toast
Sucking a lemon	Eating an ice cream cone
Changing a tire	Opening a stuck window
Putting on make-up	Catching a large fish
Dracula biting a victim	Tarzan flying through trees

Environment/Materials

Space must be adequate to have two separate teams with enough room to act out large movements and gestures. Some of the following modifications may need additional space because the children may need to practice their pantomimes in private, for example, in another room, in the hallway, or behind a barrier.

Modifications

Three modifications can be considered for grading the difficulty of the "mime phrase" game. In the first, the format of the game is the same as previously described, with teams guessing a phrase that is printed on a card. With younger children miming animals is an effective choice, as the use of animals is concrete, emotionally appealing, and relatively simple to perform. This is a good way to teach the game to young children who find it difficult to act out ideas without speech. The next step in grading the task is to mime emotions. The cards can depict such feelings as surprise, joy, anger, curiosity, and frustration; emotions are a higher order task because they are more abstract.

Another variation is to keep the group together as a single team. The children are paired in order to mime what is on the card to the total group. The practitioner considers the pairings carefully, using the individual goals as a guide. For example, a child with a problem with nonverbal communication might be paired with a child who needs experience being a leader but has adequate nonverbal skills. In another example, two children who are equally bossy can be paired to provide an opportunity to practice negotiating and problem solving.

A modification that can be used with older children is to mime vignettes and not simply phrases. For instance, instead of "buttering toast," the card could read "to prepare breakfast including making coffee, scrambling eggs, and making toast." The team gets a point for each element of the breakfast that is identified. The game can be played with one or two teams; pairs can act out the pantomime or it can be done in groups of three children. Another example of a vignette relates to social decision-making. The card can state, "Two children are playing in the living room and knock over a lamp that breaks. Act out the emotional reaction of the children and what they do." This vignette is powerful because it taps both the affective tone of the children and their social problem solving.

The role of the adult depends upon the needs of the group. The practitioner typically serves as the resource person by coaching and modeling. At times, each team may require an adult. Adults function as referees to keep track of time and help the children stay on task.

Storytelling

Purpose

Storytelling enhances communication by promoting auditory memory, discourse skills, and playful imagination. This activity helps the child be flexible in accepting the ideas of others. The variations on storytelling are limitless, and the activity is highly motivating to children. It reinforces social-emotional interaction.

Description

One variation of storytelling is termed "The Radio Show." The children sit in a circle, and one child begins to tell a story into the microphone of a tape recorder introducing characters and a situation. The microphone is passed to the next child who continues the story for a few more sentences; this process is repeated until all children have had a chance to add to the story. The children review the resulting tape as if it were a radio show. The length of the radio show can be increased by having each child speak for a longer period of time or by going around the circle two or three times. If a child introduces a story line that is tangential, the practitioner intervenes to get the story back on track.

Environment/Materials

A tape recorder with a microphone and a blank tape are the only equipment required. The room should be quiet and distraction-free.

Modifications

A variation on story telling is to make the task more visual by having pictures of three children and one or two objects such as a pet or a play object. The adult facilitates a discussion regarding who the children are, their relationship to each other, and their relationships to the objects. The practitioner then sets the scene and begins with "Once upon a time . . ."

Each child in turn picks up the story line and continues the narrative. The practitioner occasionally intervenes by introducing a social dilemma to be solved. A microphone can be used to record the story or the adult can act as a scribe.

A further modification of this activity is to create a "chapter" each time the group meets, and to create illustrations depicting each chapter. The group as a whole determines what specifically will be illustrated and who will do which pictures. This task helps the children to focus on the most relevant social aspects of the story.

Another modification is to have the children create a script by taking turns telling a story. The practitioner serves as the scribe and records the script. The children then act out the script using puppets. This is particularly useful for children who need concrete actions to represent ideas.

There are a variety of ways to conclude this activity. The children can replay the audiotape that depicts the story while holding up the pertinent pictures. This presentation can be performed for the enjoyment of the group or others such as parents or peers. Another option is to photocopy the pictures and to sequence them in the proper order of the story. Each child can color the pictures. This book can then be read to others, as the pictures provide enough of a prompt for the child to remember the story.

Collecting

Purpose

Because it can serve many goals, collecting is a common, age-appropriate leisure time activity that reflects the interests and motivations of the individual and allows children to talk about their preferences in an acceptable egocentric way. Even the simplest collection can provide prestige and pride for the child. It also provides the opportunity to work on organizational skills as the collection is assembled. The discovery of common interests with other children fosters communication and the possibility of trading items. Collecting during childhood can lead to a lifetime pursuit.

Description

Collecting is ever changing and subject to fads. Children under age 9 typically collect concrete objects such as Matchbox® cars, Beanie Babies, and rocks. Older children favor formal collections of sports or magic cards, stickers, stamps, and souvenirs from vacations.

Usually a discussion of collecting emerges from a conversation time activity in the social competence groups, and this discussion can lead to two follow-up activities. The children can bring in two to three samples of a representational collection to share and discuss with others; for example, each can bring a few stuffed toys. Or the children can bring in items from their personal collections for display and discussion. A museum show in which each child's collection is displayed for an audience can be created to allow friends or family members tour the various collections that are described by the owner.

Environment/Materials

No special requirements are needed except for floor space or tables for display.

Modifications

Some children need to be taught skills in trading and negotiating. The following five skills may need to be practiced.

1. The child may need to learn how to set the relative value of the items in a collection, that is, understanding what the items are worth.

2. The child must learn to listen to the proposals of others and to consider them even if they are different from their own expectations.

3. The child must be able to communicate personal requirements in an organized way.

4. The child must learn to negotiate flexibly in a reciprocal back and forth manner without escalating emotionally.

5. The child must be prepared for the fact that the trade may not happen and must be able to cope with the resultant disappointment and frustration.

In order to practice trading, each child is provided with multiple objects that belong to the practitioner, as trading is easiest to learn when one does not have an emotional investment in the objects to be bartered. Each child builds a collection by acquiring and then trading items. The adult models the negotiating process, and the children practice with adult feedback. Ultimately, the children have an opportunity to trade items from their personal collections.

Pit®, issued by Parker Brothers in 1973, is a collecting and trading game appropriate for children age 8 and older. This board game has a stock exchange theme in which commodities such as corn, oats, and wheat are traded. Helpful for children who are shy to learn to speak out, Pit also assists children to focus in a distracting environment. This game is exceptionally fun to play.

■ Miscellaneous Activities

Celebrations

Purpose

Celebrations are special events to recognize birthdays, holidays, achievements, and, on occasion, the completion of an intervention cycle. The children learn to participate in activities common to these events, employing their play repertoire; they also learn self-regulation and social perspective taking. Parties with peers are informal affairs with an air of spontaneous fun, and there is a loosening of expectations from the use of formal manners. Attachment to others is reinforced in a joyful atmosphere.

Description

A common complaint of parents is that a child is not invited to birthday parties or does not know how to behave at them. Social competence groups need to prepare children to participate successfully in these events. Vulnerable children experience a breakdown in behavior because these events are generally infrequent and typically chaotic.

There are familiar elements in any celebration. Formal invitations are frequently sent. There is a party atmosphere that causes a heightened state of arousal in the children, and there are typically a larger number of participants present, including strangers, than the child is comfortable encountering. During a party, some time is allocated for formal activities that may include games, but there is unstructured time when nothing is happening. Refreshments are provided that are often sweet, messy, and unfamiliar. Finally, the celebration may involve decorating the setting and giving gifts.

The use of celebrations is excellent for children from ages 5 and older can be modified for preschool children.

Environment/Materials

The space must be adequate during the preparation phase for the children to work in small groups on the different elements of the celebration, and the area must be able to accommodate the actual party. Storage is critical for all of the items that are being created. Adults have to recognize that the celebration will probably be boisterous, loud, and messy, as parties for this age group are supposed to be carefree.

Modifications

The adults identify a cause for celebration that is a natural extension of the social competence group. Possibilities include the birthday of a group member, an "unbirthday" party for all group members, the completion of a long-term project, or the completion of an instructional unit that involves a sequence of activities such as planning a party, inviting friends over, developing cooking skills, and learning how to play party games. After determining the cause for a celebration, the children decide together the elements to include in their festivities and who will be in charge of each element. This phase of preparation provides ample opportunity for mutual decision making, sequential planning, negotiating differences, and shared camaraderie. Critical for planning a celebration is the ability to take the perspective of another by understanding what will be fun for the participants. The actual celebration serves as a joyous culmination of this preparation. Based upon a group decision, the celebration could be solely for group members or include friends or family members.

Long-Term, Complex Projects

Purpose

Long-term, complex projects provide a unique experience for children, one that simulates real life decision making in adulthood. This type of activity has a direct carry over into skills needed for social competence in everyday life. These projects serve a multitude of purposes. They emphasize mutual goal setting and creating a shared outcome, and sequential problem solving helps the children think in present, past and future time. There is an evolution and repetition of prosocial skills throughout the process. The children are encouraged to think at multiple levels as they construct the project, that is, to think at the levels of social engagement, task problem solving, long-term planning, play and creative expression. Because the projects require a number of sessions to complete, the children must postpone gratification.

Long-term, complex projects are somewhat analogous to neighborhood kids who meet in June and plan a club. From this start, their activities evolve to fill a summer. These are truly memorable experiences — "Remember the summer we made the tree house?" A hallmark of these complex projects is the degree of imagination that is involved; these experiences are unique, personal, and not commercially available. In contemporary society there seems to be less of an opportunity for children to hang out in an unsupervised environment in which they participate in imaginative play, and this experience differs from hanging out at the mall, going to a soccer game, or playing karate.

Description

The following discussion is a prototype of long-term, complex projects, and the process is described in some detail in order to convey the idea of the group experience over time.

A social competence group composed of nine children with and without identified special needs was led by a social worker and an occupational therapist in an after school program for children ages 6 and 7. At the beginning of the 8-week session, there was a discussion of the activities in which the children were participating for the summer. A number of children mentioned going to the beach, and this was the catalyst for the group deciding to build a ship that they could play in. The children designed the ship, divided up the tasks, and worked in small groups. The result was a life-sized ship made of cardboard that had sails, portholes, a flag for each group member, a mast head, an anchor with a rope, and a helm. After completing the ship, the children created an ocean composed of sea creatures of all sorts, seashells, and seaweed. Next, they completed the scene by constructing a beach that contained shells, a lemonade stand, palm trees, and waves washing against the shore.

The construction phase was over by the 4th week, and the children spent the next 4 weeks enjoying imaginative play. They were divided into small groups and rotated through three stations, namely the ship, the beach, and the ocean. The groups played dramatically around specific themes. The beach people made sand castles, played catch, collected seashells, and sold lemonade. The ocean people fished, swam, and dived for treasure, while the ship people played pirates, got lost, and managed a storm. The practitioners would suggest a play theme only if the children could not generate one on their own and intervened selectively to help the children to sustain the momentum of the play. On occasion, playful behavior was modeled. Most of the time, however, the practitioners simply observed and encouraged the children. After two weeks the groups started joining each other by extending the play themes. For instance, the ship people provided a tour of the boat for the beach people and the ocean people capsized their dingy and were rescued by the beach people. Eventually there were no boundaries between stations, but rather a free flow of children from one location to another driven by the unfolding drama.

Environment

This activity requires a lot of space. Unless the project can stay intact over sequential weeks, it must be readily dismantled and reassembled week by week; therefore, storage between sessions becomes an important issue. During the play phase the project has to be spread apart so that there is ample space for the children to interact and follow their imaginations. Props can add a lot of interest to the play. In this project a cardboard box served as a dingy, a large pillow was an island in the ocean, a yardstick served as a fishing pole, and a beach ball was used for catch. As the drama proceeds, the noise level can escalate.

Modifications

For children with problems in motor control, the construction tasks can be made easier by having items such as seashells pre-drawn so only coloring is required; these children can also use magazine pictures as models for ideas to copy. Children who are gifted and very creative can be given full license to explore their imaginations; for example, they can design and decorate sea creatures that are scientifically accurate for different ocean depths. In addition to the boat theme, there are unlimited options for other types of complex projects such as the jungle, mountains, the zoo, school, town, museums, and super hero fantasies.

Associated Issues

This chapter addresses four critical issues related to conducting a social competence program. First, sample illustrations are provided for extending the use of our social competence approach based on the conceptual framework, then working effectively with families is discussed. Next, numerous strategies are offered to strengthen generalization of learning by the children. Finally, evaluation data are presented suggesting the positive effectiveness of our intervention approach.

Illustrations of the Social Competence Approach

There are many ways that the practitioner can use our conceptual framework to promote the social adequacy of children. The approach described in this book is very versatile and has many applications; for instance, school-based practitioners may incorporate elements from this model into their services, thus adding a social interactive component to the child's intervention. The following examples are representative of opportunities for the creative application of our approach in a school. These examples can be replicated in other settings such as Scouts, clubs, and private practice clinics.

Skill Development Groups

One can enhance skill development groups in school settings by incorporating social competence goals. For instance, occupational therapists often run fine motor groups focusing on handwriting. The social dimension of this type of group can be promoted by having the children write a story together and illustrate it in a booklet. In this collaborative exchange the children are working on communication while listening to the ideas of others and sharing thoughts. Self-regulation is practiced by learning to wait and not blurt out ideas. In addition, prosocial skills are reinforced by turn-taking, soliciting ideas, and engaging in shared decision making. Having a small group of children together can facilitate skill development through shared experience and competition. Similar group experiences with a social component could be reading, math, or speech and language groups.

Classroom Play Activity

The regular routine of the classroom provides many opportunities for fostering social behaviors in a naturalistic manner. The children are learning competencies embedded in the context in which they are to be used. For example, a teacher had six children in her class who had varying delays in their spontaneous play. These children did not notice or imitate or model the behaviors of their typically developing peers. She grouped the targeted children together during free playtime and read them an original story that was designed to describe 2–3 play possibilities with selected toys. The social story with its visual illustrations served to prepare the children regarding ways to play with the toys and each other, and the teacher coached the children using the book to help them maintain order during their play. In using this approach, she was addressing the play and social development of the children.

Physical Education

Athletic programs can be tailored to achieve physical and social outcomes simultaneously. As a child's motor competence increases, social competence may improve, and with enhanced strength and coordination, the child can shift attention and effort to the social side of games and sports. This progression often requires a carefully graded skill development program. For example, Harry wanted to be able to play basketball with his peers but could not dribble or shoot the ball, let alone grasp the rules of the game. His physical education teacher introduced him to ball management beginning with a two-handed dribble, then a one-handed dribble, later moving on to passing and stealing the ball, and finally to free shooting. Once the individual skills were mastered, Harry and two peers began practicing specific game strategies and their related rules one rule at a time. After three strategies were learned, the group was challenged to a mock game against the teacher. In this scenario Harry acquired motor skills and expanded his play repertoire to include cooperative play in the team sport of basketball.

Collaborative Learning

A common teaching method is the use of collaborative learning situations in the classroom, in which children are clustered in small groups to work on shared projects. Children with problems in social competence typically find these experiences very stressful and unsuccessful. They may be too bossy and impulsive, unable to communicate their ideas within the fast pace of peer conversation, unable to compromise and negotiate group decisions, and too disorganized to carry their workload. As a result, true collaboration is undermined.

An example promoting successful collaboration involved a teacher who used the group assignment of creating a newsletter on a computer. She guaranteed motivation by having the newsletter focus on the personal lives of the children. The social agenda began with rules about how the group members would conduct themselves. In addition, the children made group decisions about the letterhead and its color, the formatting of the articles, and other design elements. To facilitate interaction, group members interviewed peers in the process of developing articles on topics such as experiences during summer vacation, reviews of recent movies, website reviews, and a calendar of school events. Articles were jointly written on the computer, illustrations were chosen, and the layout finalized. The teacher provided technical support and instruction when needed and facilitated the group process.

Peer Tutor

Assigning a buddy to a child with social difficulties can be a helpful intervention technique. Typically, the tutor has social abilities that the targeted child would like to emulate. The two can spend time together in the classroom and during unstructured time such as the lunch period and recess. The tutor receives instruction in the goals to be addressed with the child. For instance, with a young child a tutor may model how to engage in pretend play by using learned scripts to invite a child to play and to elaborate on the fantasy. The tutor is encouraged to be persistent so that the child will remain involved in the play. In the case of an older child who alienates peers by his behavior and appearance, a buddy could be chosen who is attractive and popular. The targeted child can accept advice from this tutor because of his status in the social group, and because the child wants to emulate the tutor's style and manner.

Coaching During the School Day

Coaching is based on the adult's social goals for a particular child. Throughout the natural flow of the school day, the teacher and other practitioners intervene as opportunities arise. A pre-established word or a gesture can be used to signal the need for a desired behavior. As this technique is used in context intermittently throughout the day, this approach promotes generalization of learning across situations. Coaching in the natural environment is the logical follow up to intensive group work.

The preceding examples demonstrate numerous ways that our approach can be implemented in a school environment. As described in Chapters 10 and 11, social competence groups can be conducted in the classroom or in a pullout format. Variations of this group model can also be applied to the gym, lunchroom, or playground settings.

Working With Families

Families are critical in fostering the social development of children. However, few social skills programs have systematically addressed family needs and incorporated parent involvement. This is a missed opportunity because parents are particularly suited to assist the child to integrate and transfer newly acquired skills from one context to another. Family support services can be tailored to expand parental understanding of social development and the challenges faced by children with social difficulties. They can also provide specific strategies parents may use in promoting their child's social effectiveness. These services can decrease the sense of isolation felt by many parents by having opportunities to share with others who have similar needs and concerns, as well as increase the parents' knowledge of relevant community resources and social support networks.

There are numerous methods for fostering parent participation. The following services have been used in our practice with success.

- **Identification of the Child's Status.** As discussed in Chapter 8, parents provide vital information about their child's needs and resources through interviews and questionnaires.

- **Collaborative Goal Setting.** As described in Chapter 9, parents share in writing personalized intervention goals for their child.

- **Parent Discussion Groups.** Parents can meet while their children are in the program or special group meetings can be scheduled. Content is commonly focused on addressing emotional issues such as feelings about being a parent of a child with special needs and concerns about the child's problem, or expanding knowledge of intervention strategies including techniques for behavior management and solving conflicts. Parents determine the topics to be addressed and the format for the sessions.

- **Observation of the Child.** Parents can observe the child's intervention through a one-way mirror or videotape. In general, the parents are not allowed to observe first-hand because their presence interferes with the group process and changes the group dynamics. On occasion, a brief visit by the parents may be acceptable if a practitioner is available to describe what is happening.

- **Parent Conferences.** These conferences can be held with or without the child present. The focus is on sharing information, providing intervention suggestions, strategies for generalizing skills, and technical assistance regarding next steps. Parents are often in need of additional professional and community resources. Plans for the social competence group are influenced by the information that emerges in the parent conferences.

- **Evaluation of Child's Progress.** Parents often complete questionnaires regarding the progress of their child. This information contributes to the reassessment process and the setting of new goals.

- **Problem Solving Special Events.** The practitioner works with the parent to create strategies to make special events successful. Of particular importance are birthday parties, sleepovers, play dates, and extended family gatherings. All of these events can be very challenging for the child and family to socially navigate.

- **Coaching Parents.** Many parents have questions regarding their parenting style and their child's behavior. The practitioner has an important role in providing information and resources to enhance the knowledge of the parents, who often need concrete strategies for managing the child's behavior.

Generalization

A major criticism of social skills training programs is the poor generalization of skills and limited maintenance of skills over time. In evaluation studies, the children may demonstrate immediate gains, but these changes in behavior are not demonstrated in day-to-day functional living. We have implemented six major strategies to address these challenges.

1. Learning in the social competence program is carefully embedded in naturalistic peer activities, and this activity-based interaction is the primary thrust of our intervention. These activities provide opportunities for spontaneous, internally motivated interaction to occur, interaction that is not dependent on adults; in contrast, standard social skills training focuses on teaching discrete lessons. The closer the intervention is to the desired functional outcomes, the stronger the carryover of learning will be.

2. The use of multiple intervention techniques enhances social learning more than a single strategy does. Our approach uses coaching, modeling, direct teaching, and naturalistic activities as well as other techniques to reinforce learning.

3. The program addresses the feelings and concerns of the children and guides them in solving their daily social problems. Practice and the accompanying development of self-confidence result from the children completing community-based assignments such as telephoning a peer, planning with a friend what to play during recess, or applying strategies to cope with teasing at the bus stop.

4. Peer tutors are often assigned to encourage carryover of learning from the group experience to everyday realities of the school and neighborhood. These tutors can take advantage of incidental learning opportunities throughout the child's day, and social skills are therefore reinforced in their natural context.

5. Along with participation in a social competence group, children are encouraged to participate in neighborhood activities such as soccer, volleyball, scouts, swim team, and religious groups. The practitioners provide needed consultation to assure that the children will have a successful transitional experience, and generalization of learning is therefore transferred to the more community-based activities.

6. Practitioners from the social competence program work closely with parents and other personnel to assure that competencies and skills acquired in the therapeutic group are recognized and supported in other settings. Thus, desired skills are practiced and repeated in a variety of situations and circumstances. Likewise, peers are assisted to recognize the improved abilities of the children who formally participated in the social competence program. Thus, there is less likelihood a past history of social incompetence will continue to stigmatize a child.

The practitioner should implement a number of strategies for encouraging generalization of learning across situations. Otherwise there is the risk that gains achieved in the social competence group will not transfer to the child's moment-to-moment social world.

Evaluation Study

A descriptive evaluation study examined the impact of social competence groups using our conceptual framework. Eighteen intervention groups were conducted in 16-session treatment cycles over a period of 2½ years, with fall, spring, and summer cycles being held. Typically, 2–3 groups were scheduled each cycle. The social competence groups followed the program format and activities described in Chapters 10 and 11. Each group was facilitated by two practitioners and served approximately eight children. The presenting needs of the children in each group determined which two professional disciplines would be involved, with practitioners drawn from occupational therapy, speech and language pathology, special education, social work, and psychology. Each group had common therapeutic goals that were shared by all members, as well as individual goals that were developed for each child.

A total of 120 children, 103 boys and 17 girls, participated in the various groups over the multi-year period; 37% were ages 5–7, 40% were ages 7–9 , and 23% were ages 10–12. The children were typically classified by their local school district as neurologically impaired, perceptually impaired, or communication handicapped, with the most common medical diagnosis being attention deficit disorder, with or without hyperactivity. Thirty of the children did not have a medical diagnosis or educational classification, but were regularly developing children who had social difficulties.

Pre- and post-testing of the children was performed during each treatment cycle. The SSRS (Gresham & Elliott, 1990) was administered as a norm-referenced instrument to assess social skills and problem behaviors. The social skills dimension addressed the three subscales of cooperation, assertion, and self-control, and the problem behavior dimension addressed the three subscales of externalizing problems, internalizing problems, and hyperactivity. A goal attainment measure was also used. The parents and practitioners determined the achievement of individual intervention goals at the end of the child's treatment cycle, and the goals were rated according to "achieved," "in progress" or partially mastered, and "not achieved." Finally, parents completed a written survey that addressed such areas as satisfaction with the program, their view of the child's progress, and the child's social performance at school, home, and community.

Pre- and post-testing of the 120 children indicated that they improved in their social competence. Using the SSRS, significant increases in social skills were realized as rated by practitioners ($F = 140.94$; $df = 1, 114$; $p = .000$) and parents ($F = 25.16$; $df = 1, 114$; $p = .000$). Likewise, significant decreases in rating scores for problem behaviors were reported by practitioners ($F = 40.04$; $df = 1, 114$; $p = .000$) and parents ($F = 11.68$; $df = 1, 114$; $p = .001$).

Results from this instrument indicated a more significant increase in overall social skills ratings than a decrease in overall problem behavior ratings. In general, eliminating unwanted behavior such as aggression and impulsivity was more resistant to change than learning new social skills. Interestingly, the practitioners tended to rate the children as more competent than the parents rated them and also recorded a higher rate of child progress. However, both parents and practitioners felt that the children made significant progress in social skills and reduced problem behaviors as a result of participation in the social competence group.

Of the total of 314 intervention goals that were established for the children during the period of the study, 94% were rated as "achieved" or "partially mastered" at the end of the treatment cycle; only 6% were rated "not achieved." Improvements were particularly noted in the ability to: follow rules, use appropriate body language and personal space, share experiences and ideas, regulate emotional state, maintain task engagement, and take turns in conversation. The parent survey documented the following major community-based outcomes: an increase in personal comfort in group settings, number of friends, and motivation in school accompanied by a decrease in self-consciousness, sibling rivalry, and fighting with peers. Further evaluation studies need to be conducted controlling for different variables. However, the results of this multi-year study support the effectiveness of our social competence approach.

Appendix A.1

Self-Awareness Assessment

Child's Name: _____ Date: _____

	Rarely	Sometimes	Often
1. I can make friends easily.	☐	☐	☐
2. Once I make a friend, the friendship lasts a long time.	☐	☐	☐
3. I notice when things need to be done without reminders.	☐	☐	☐
4. I know what to do in different settings without reminders from adults.	☐	☐	☐
5. When decisions need to be shared with one or more friends, I can think up at least two different choices that will work out and please everyone.	☐	☐	☐
6. I recognize what I do well, so-so, or poorly.	☐	☐	☐
7. I am able to show confidence in what I do well and my ability to try new things.	☐	☐	☐
8. I know what I don't do as well as others and I don't mind that they are better at these things than I am.	☐	☐	☐
9. I notice when someone needs help or company and offer it in a way that makes them feel good.	☐	☐	☐
10. When I need assistance I am able to ask someone in a way that will get me the help I want.	☐	☐	☐

Self-Awareness Assessment printed here with permission by Wilma J. Dorman © 2002.

Copyright © 2002 by Therapy Skill Builders, a Harcourt Assessment Company. All rights reserved. Promoting Social Competence, G. Gordon Williamson and Wilma J. Dorman / ISBN 076160216X / 1-800-228-0752. This page is reproducible.

Appendix A.2

Child and Family Profile

Child's Name: _____ Date of Birth: _____

Parents/Guardian: _____

Siblings: _____

_____

_____

Health History: Please check any of the following that apply to your child:

☐ Hospitalizations _____

    When? _____

☐ Surgeries _____

    When? _____

☐ Sleep Problems _____

    At what age and how often? (e.g., every night, once a week) _____

☐ Bed Wetting _____

    At what age and how often? _____

☐ Medical Problems _____

    Include communicable diseases (please list) child has had (e.g., chicken pox) _____

_____

☐ Is there any family history of the preceding medical problems? (e.g., father or mother has asthma)

_____

Please answer the following questions in a few sentences. This information will help us to know your child better and to evaluate the appropriate services to offer.

Background

    1.   When did you first become concerned? _____

    2.   Why are you interested in services now? _____

    3.   Have other people expressed similar concerns? (e.g., teacher, spouse, grandparents, friends)

_____

4. Has your child expressed or shown concerns about peer relationships? Explain.

_____

5. Have you sought this type of service (or a similar one) at another time? _____

_____

6. What similarities do you see in your child's ability to socialize compared to other family members and other children? What differences? _____

_____

Parenting

1. Parenting is one of the most difficult responsibilities. Please list some of your particular parenting strengths.

_____

2. List any parenting skills that you would like to develop or enhance. _____

_____

3. What goals would you like to accomplish for yourself as a parent by participating in the program?

_____

4. List three behaviors of your child that are difficult to manage. _____

_____

   a. Cite some situations where they occur. _____

   b. How do you respond to these behaviors? (e.g., ignore, yell, hit, time out) _____

   c. How does your child respond to these attempts to discipline? _____

Child

1. State three things you like about your child. _____

_____

_____

_____

2. State three things you would like to be different about your child. _____

_____

_____

_____

3. Does your child prefer playing alone or with friends? _____

4. Give a recent example of a problem your child had with a peer. _____

_____

5. How was it handled? _____

_____

6. What activities does your child enjoy playing in the following situations:

Alone _____

_____

With friends _____

_____

With family members _____

_____

Groups

1. How many friends does your child have? _____

2. Where? _____

Best Friend? _____

3. When dealing with a stressful or difficult situation, my child is likely to:

☐ Withdraw

☐ Become aggressive

☐ Act silly

☐ Be calm and reasonable

☐ Act impulsively

☐ Other

4. In which of the following situations does your child most comfortably interact with peers?

☐ With younger children

☐ With older children

☐ One to one

☐ Small to large groups

☐ Structured situations

☐ Unstructured situations

☐ Table top activities

☐ Outdoor activities

Appendix A.3

Identification of Social Difficulties

Child's Name: _____ Date: _____

Parents's Name: _____

	Rarely	Sometimes	Often
1. My child tends to play alone or with younger children.	☐	☐	☐
2. My child has trouble making and keeping friends.	☐	☐	☐
3. My child does not play the games or participate in the activities that peers enjoy.	☐	☐	☐
4. My child's difficulty with impulsivity, distractability, or hyperactivity often has an impact on social situations.	☐	☐	☐
5. My child behaves intrusively or inflexibly and this undermines social relationships.	☐	☐	☐
6. My child has problems in social situations due to limited communication (e.g., starting and maintaining conversations; turn taking; informing and persuading others).	☐	☐	☐
7. My child does not acknowledge the point of view of others or does not respect it.	☐	☐	☐
8. My child has few strategies for solving social problems (e.g., knowing what to do when interactions "get stuck").	☐	☐	☐
9. When social difficulties are encountered, my child rarely takes responsibility for contributing to them.	☐	☐	☐
10. My child has little awareness of the consequences of social actions.	☐	☐	☐

Appendix A.4

Teacher Impression Scale

Child's Name: _____ Date: _____

Teacher: _____ Subject Number: _____

Please read each item below and rate the degree to which it describes the child's behavior in your classroom program. If you have not seen the child perform a particular skill or behavior, circle 1, indicating Never. If the child frequently performs the described skill or behavior, circle 5, indicating Frequently. If the child performs this behavior in between these two extremes, circle 2, 3, or 4 indicating your best estimate of the rate of occurrence of the skill.

1 = Never Performs Skill
5 = Frequently Performs Skill

Circle only one number for each skill. Do not mark between numbers.

1 2 3 4 5   1. The child converses appropriately.

1 2 3 4 5   2. The child takes turns when playing.

1 2 3 4 5   3. The child plays cooperatively.

1 2 3 4 5   4. The child varies social behavior appropriately.

1 2 3 4 5   5. The child is persistent at social attempts.

1 2 3 4 5   6. The child spontaneously responds to peers.

1 2 3 4 5   7. The child appears to have fun.

1 2 3 4 5   8. Peers interacting with the child appear to have fun.

1 2 3 4 5   9. The child continues an interaction once it has begun.

1 2 3 4 5   10. Peers seek out the child for social play.

1 2 3 4 5   11. The child uses appropriate social behavior to begin an interaction.

1 2 3 4 5   12. The child enters play activities without disrupting the group.

1 2 3 4 5   13. The child suggests new play ideas for a play group.

1 2 3 4 5   14. The child smiles appropriately at peers during play.

1 2 3 4 5   15. The child shares play materials with peers.

1 2 3 4 5   16. The child engages in play activities where social interaction might occur.

From Samuel Odom and Scott McConnell, *Playtime/Social Time: Organizing your Classroom to Build Interaction Skills*, 1993. p.13. Reprinted by permission.

Appendix A.5

Components of Social Competence

Child: _____ Date of Birth: _____

Person Completing Form: _____ Date of Evalutaion: _____

Please rate the child's social behavior in the following areas by circling the appropriate number.

Social and Play Behavior	Rarely	Sometimes	Often
1. Takes advantage of opportunities to play with others.	1	2	3
2. Plays with appropriate peers.	1	2	3
3. Participates in a wide variety of games and activities.	1	2	3
4. Demonstrates playfulness.	1	2	3
5. Demonstrates age appropriate social play (solitary to cooperative play).	1	2	3

Self-Regulation	Rarely	Sometimes	Often
1. Looks at people appropriately when listening and speaking.	1	2	3
2. Uses appropriate body language and personal space.	1	2	3
3. Pays attention.	1	2	3
4. Uses voice appropriately (tone, volume, pitch).	1	2	3
5. Keeps control of emotions when upset.	1	2	3

Communication	Rarely	Sometimes	Often
1. Starts a conversation with peers.	1	2	3
2. Keeps a conversation going.	1	2	3
3. Takes turns during a conversation.	1	2	3
4. Uses appropriate language when speaking (words, sentence structure).	1	2	3
5. Expresses self clearly (gets the message across to the listener).	1	2	3
6. Starts conversation again after it breaks down (at time of silence or disagreement).	1	2	3

7. Uses language for the following purposes:	Rarely	Sometimes	Often
a. makes requests	1	2	3
b. describes events	1	2	3
c. comments	1	2	3
d. shares information	1	2	3
e. explains or justifies opinions and ideas	1	2	3
f. protests or expresses dissatisfaction.	1	2	3
g. disagrees	1	2	3

Social Decision Making

	Rarely	Sometimes	Often
1. Notices when things are not going well.	1	2	3
2. Considers the ideas and feelings of others.	1	2	3
3. Contributes ideas for possible solutions.	1	2	3
4. Describes possible consequences for the solutions.	1	2	3
5. Makes an effort to carry out the chosen solution.	1	2	3
6. Tries problem-solving process again if previous efforts fail.	1	2	3

References

Allport, G. W. (1937). *Personality: A psychological interpretation.* New York: Holt Co.

Beelman, A., Pfingsten, U., & Losel, F. (1994). Effects of training social competence in children: A meta-analysis of recent evaluation studies. *Journal of Clinical Child Psychology, 23*, 260–271.

Breines, E. B. (1995). *Occupational therapy activities from clay to computers: Theory and practice.* Philadelphia: F. A. Davis.

Cassidy, J. (1997). Attachment theory. In S. Greenspan, S. Wieder, & J. Osofsky (Eds.), *Handbook of child and adolescent psychiatry,* (Vol. 1), pp. 236–250. New York: John Wiley & Sons.

Clark, R. (1985). *The parent-child early relational assessment instrument and manual.* Madison, WI: University of Wisconsin Medical School, Department of Psychiatry.

Clark, R., Paulson, A., & Conlin, S. (1993). *Assessment of Development Status and Parent-Infant Relationships: The Theraputic Process of Evaluation.* In C.H. Zeanah, Jr. (Ed.) *Handbook of Infant Mental Health* (pp. 191–209). New York: Guilford Press.

Cole, M. B. (1993). *Group dynamics in occupational therapy: The theoretical basis and practice application of group treatment.* Thorofare, NJ: SLACK.

Denham, S., & Almeida, M. (1987). Children's social problem solving skills, behavioral adjustment, and interventions: A meta-analysis evaluating theory and practice. *Journal of Applied Developmental Psychology, 8*, 391–409.

Dorman, W. J., & Williamson, G. G. (2000). *Identification of social difficulties questionnaire.* Unpublished manuscript.

Dorman, W. J. (1999). *Self-awareness assessment.* Unpublished manuscript.

Elias, M. J., & Clabby, J. F. (1989). *Social decision-making skills: A curriculum guide for the elementary grades.* Rockville, MD: Aspen.

Elksnin, L. K., & Elksnin, N. (1998). Teaching social skills to students with learning and behavior problems. *Intervention in school and clinic, 33*(3), 131–140.

Florey, L. L., & Greene, S. (1997). Play in middle childhood: A focus on children with behavior and emotional disorders. In L. D. Parham & L. S. Fazio (Eds.), *Play in occupational therapy for children* (pp. 126–143). St. Louis, MO: Mosby.

Goldsmith, H. H., Buss, A. H., Plomin, R., Rothbart, M. K., Thomas, A., Chess, S., Hinde, R. A., & McCall, R. B. (1987). Roundtable: What is temperament? Four approaches. *Child Development, 58*, 505–529.

Goldstein, S., & Goldstein, M. (1995). *A teacher's guide: Attention-deficit hyperactivity disorder in children* (3rd ed.). Salt Lake City, UT: Neurology, Learning and Behavior Center.

Goldstein, S., & Braswell, L. (1995). *Understanding and managing children's classroom behavior.* New York: John Wiley & Sons.

Gresham, F. M. (1998). Social skills training: Should we raze, remodel, or rebuild? *Behavioral Disorders: Journal of the Council for Children with Behavioral Disorders, 24*(1), 19–25.

Gresham, F. M., & Elliott, S. N. (1990). *Social skills rating system.* Circle Pines, MN: American Guidance Service.

Gresham, F. M., & MacMillan, D. L. (1997). Social competence and affective characteristics of students with mild disabilities. *Review of Educational Research, 67*(4), 377–415.

Gresham, F. M., Sugai, G., & Horner, R. H. (2001). Outcomes of social skills training for students with high-incidence disabilities. *Exceptional Children: Journal of the International Council for Exceptional Children, 67*(3), 331–344.

Gutstein, S. E. (2000). *Autism aspergers: Solving the relationship puzzle.* Arlington, TX: Future Horizons.

Haring, N. (1992). The context of social competence: Relations, relationships, and generalization. In S. Odom, S. McConnell, & M. McElvoy (Eds.), *Social competence of young children with disabilities: Issues and strategies for intervention* (pp. 307–320). Baltimore: Brookes.

Hetherington, E. M., & Parke, R. D. (1986). *Child psychology: a contemporary viewpoint* (3rd ed.). (p. 682). New York: McGraw-Hill.

Hildebrand, V. (1975). *Guiding young children.* New York: Macmillan.

Hull, K., Venn, M. L., Lee, J. M., & Van Buren, M. (2000). Passports for learning in inclusive settings. In S. Sandall & M. Ostrosky (Eds.), *Young exceptional children: Natural environments and inclusion* (pp. 69–77). Monograph Series No. 2. Denver, CO: Division for Early Childhood/Council for Exceptional Children.

Kavale, K. A., & Forness, S. R. (1996). Social skills deficits and learning disabilities: A meta-analysis. *Journal of Learning Disabilities, 29*(3), 226–237.

Kelly, J.E. & Barnard, K.E. (2000). Assessment of parent-child interaction: Implications for early intervention. In J.P. Shakoff & S.J. Meisets (Eds.) *Handbook of Early Childhood Intervention* (pp. 258–289). New York: Cambridge University Press.

Knox, S., & Mailloux, Z. (1997). Play as treatment and treatment through play. In B. E. Chandler (Ed.), *The essence of play: A child's occupation.* Bethesda, MD: American Occupational Therapy Association.

Kupersmidt, J., Coie, J., & Dodge, K. (1990). The role of peer relationships in the development of disorder. In S. Asher & J. Coie (Eds.), *Peer rejection in childhood* (pp. 274–308). New York: Cambridge University Press.

La Greca, A., & Stone, W. (1990). Children with learning disabilities: The role of achievement in social, personal, and behavioral functioning. In H. L. Swanson & B. Keogh (Eds.), *Learning disabilities: Theoretical and research issues* (pp. 333–352). Hillsdale, NJ: Erlbaum.

Lazarus, R., & Folkman, S. (1984). *Stress, appraisal and coping.* New York: Springer.

Levine, M. D. (1987). *Developmental variation and learning disorders.* Cambridge, MA: Educators Publishing Service.

Liberman, R. P. (1982). Social skills assessment. *Schizophrenia Bulletin, 8*, 1.

Odom, S. L., & McConnell, S. R. (1993). *Play time/social time.* Tucson, AZ: Communication Skill Builders.

Parham, L. D., & Primeau, L. A. (1997). Play and occupational therapy. In L. D. Parham & L. S. Fazio (Eds.), *Play in occupational therapy for children* (pp. 2–21). St. Louis, MO: Mosby.

Parten, M. B. (1932). Social participation among preschool children. *Journal of Abnormal Psychology, 27*, 243–269.

Pugmire-Stoy, M. C. (1992). *Spontaneous play in early childhood.* Albany, NY: Delmar.

Quinn, M. M., Kavale, K. A., Mathur, S. R., Rutherford, R. B. Jr., & Forness, S. R. (1999). A meta-analysis of social skill interventions for students with emotional or behavioral disorders. *Journal of Emotional and Behavioral Disorders, 7*, 54–64.

Rothbart, M. K., & Derryberry, D. (1981). Development of individual differences in temperament. In M. E. Lamb & A. L. Brown (Eds.), *Advances in developmental psychology,* (Vol. 1), pp. 37–86. Hillsdale, NJ: Lawrence Erlbaum Associates.

Rutherford, R. B., Jr. (1997). Why doesn't social skills training work? *CEC Today,* July, 14. Reston, VA: The Council for Exceptional Children.

Schumaker, J. B., & Hazel, J. S. (1984). Social skills assessment and training for the learning disabled: Who's on first and what's on second? Part I. *Journal of Learning Disabilities, 17*, 422–431.

Selman, R. L., & Jacquette, D. (1978). Stability and oscillation in interpersonal awareness: A clinical-developmental analysis. In C. B. Keasy (Ed.), *The XXV Nebraska symposium on motivation.* University of Nebraska Press.

Sheridan, S. M., Hungelmann, A., & Maughan, D. P. (1999). A contextualized framework for social skills assessment, intervention, and generalization. *School Psychology Review, 28*(1), 84–103.

Thomas, A., & Chess, S. (1977). *Temperament and development.* New York: Brunner/Mazel.

Vaughn, S., & Haager, D. (1994). Social competence as a multifaceted construct: how do students with learning disabilities fare? *Learning Disability Quarterly: Journal of the Division for Children with Learning Disabilities, 17*, 253–267.

Walker, H. M., Colvin, G., & Ramsey, E. (1995). *Antisocial behavior in school: Strategies and best practices.* Pacific Grove, CA: Brooks/Cole.

Walker, H. M., & McConnell, S. R. (1995). *Walker-McConnell scale of social competence and school adjustment.* Elementary version. San Diego, CA: Singular.

Westby, C. E. (1991). A scale for assessing children's pretend play. In C. E. Schaefer, K. Gitlin, & A. Sandgrund (Eds.), *Play diagnosis and assessment* (pp. 131–161). New York: John Wiley & Sons.

Williamson, G. G. (2000). *Child and family profile.* Unpublished manuscript.

Williamson, G. G. (2000). *Components of social competence observation scale.* Unpublished manuscript.

Wood, M. M., Combs, C., Gunn, A., & Weller, D. (1986). *Developmental therapy in the classroom: Methods for teaching students with social, emotional, or behavioral handicaps* (2nd ed.). Austin, TX: Pro-Ed.

Zaragoza, N., Vaughn, S., & McIntosh, R. (1991). Social skills interventions and children with behavior problems: A review. *Behavioral Disorders, 16,* 260–275.

Zeanah, C. H., Mammen, O. K., & Lieberman, A. F. (1993). Disorders in attachment. In C. H. Zeanah, Jr. (Ed.), *Handbook of infant mental health* (pp. 332–349). New York: Guilford Press.

Zeitlin, S., & Williamson, G. G. (1994). Coping in young children: Early intervention practices to enhance adaptive behavior and resilience. Baltimore: Paul H. Brookes.